Praise for *Toxic Sludge Is Good For You*

"The best w[...]e[...] [...]eading."
Robert McC[...] [...]t Theirs

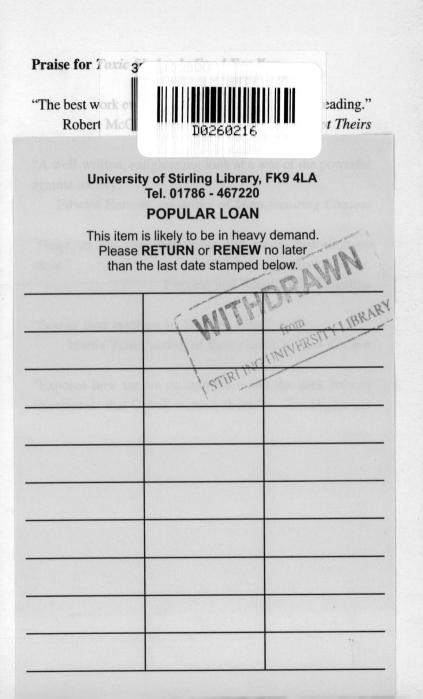

ALSO BY SHELDON RAMPTON AND JOHN STAUBER

TRUST US, WE'RE EXPERTS!

TOXIC SLUDGE IS GOOD FOR YOU!

MAD COW U.S.A.

Weapons of Mass Deception

The Uses of Propaganda in Bush's War on Iraq

SHELDON RAMPTON
and JOHN STAUBER

ROBINSON
London

While the authors have made every effort to provide accurate telephone numbers and Internet addresses at the time of publication, neither the publisher nor the authors assume any reponsibility for errors, or for changes that occur after publication.

Constable & Robinson Ltd
3 The Lanchesters
162 Fulham Palace Road
London W6 9ER
www.constablerobinson.com

First published in the USA by Jeremy P. Tarcher/Penguin, 2003

First published in the UK by Robinson,
an imprint of Constable & Robinson Ltd, 2003

Copyright © Center for Media and Democracy 2003

A copy of the British Library Cataloguing in
Publication data is available from the British Library

ISBN 1-84119-837-4

Book design by Lovedog Studio

Printed and bound in the EU

3 5 7 9 10 8 6 4

Contents

Acknowledgments

We thank our employer, the nonprofit educational organization Center for Media & Democracy, and the individuals and nonprofit foundations that have supported its work since 1993. This book is part of the Center's unique mission of investigating propaganda as it is waged by corporations and governments. For information on the Center, visit its website at www.prwatch .org, or contact its office: 520 University Avenue, Suite 310, Madison, Wisconsin, 53703; phone: (608) 260-9713.

Many thanks to our wonderful colleague Laura Miller, the associate editor of the Center's quarterly *PR Watch*, who has been like a third author of this book, contributing research and writing, especially in the chapters "War Is Sell" and "Doublespeak."

Thanks especially to our editor Mitch Horowitz for his invaluable advice, encouragement and good sense. Thanks also to publisher Joel Fotinos of Jeremy P. Tarcher for the opportunity to write it. We thank John Kelly Groves, Tarcher/Penguin publicist, and Tom Grady, our wise agent and adviser.

The following organizations and individuals have helped us with ideas, comments, research and other support: Grant Abert, Asif Agha, Harriet Barlow, Aarick Beher, Laura Berger, Gordon Brand, Bob Burton, Joe Davis, Pamela Frorer, Grodzins Fund, Edward Goldsmith, Earl Hood, Linda Jameson, Jim Kavanagh, Oliver Kellhammer, Donna Balkan Litowitz, Robert Litowitz, Kevin McCauley, Laiman Mai, Marianne Manilov, Joe Mendelson, Dave Merritt, The Middle East Research and Information Project, David Miller, Gretta Wing Miller, Tim Nelson, Dan Perkins, Scott Robbe, Abby Rockefeller, Andy Rowell, Debra Schwarze, Paul Alan Smith, John H. Stauber, Chris Toensing, Nancy Ward, the Winslow Foundation, Walda Wood and Margie Zilic.

John thanks his colleague Sheldon for shouldering most of the burden of writing this book. John dedicates it to three activist friends who have passed on but whose inspiration remains: Alex Kurki, Billee Shoecraft and Tom Saunders.

Introduction: Liberation Day

As U.S. TANKS stormed into Baghdad on April 9, 2003, television viewers in the United States got their first feel-good moment of the war—a chance to witness the toppling of a giant statue of Iraqi dictator Saddam Hussein.

Americans channel-flipping over breakfast among Fox, CNN and CBS all saw the same images, broadcast live from Baghdad's Firdos Square. For those who missed it in the morning, the images were continually replayed on cable news throughout the day, and newspapers carried front-page color photos.

A crowd of jubilant Iraqis had climbed onto the statue, thrown a noose around its neck and tried to pull it down. A man with a sledgehammer began pounding at its concrete base. Others took turns, but the statue was too big and the base too massive, so the U.S. Marines moved in with an armored vehicle and a chain. The soldiers had brought along an American flag, which they passed up to Private Ed Chin, the soldier working to affix the chain around Saddam's neck. Chin draped the flag over Saddam's face, but the gesture stirred a ripple of the wrong kind of feeling from the Iraqis. An Iraqi flag was found to replace the American flag. The crane began to pull, and Saddam's statue first bent from its pedestal and then snapped completely, to roars of approval from the crowd, which surged forward to stomp on its remains, kicking and spitting on the rubble. Whooping, they dragged its head through the street.

In the months leading up to the invasion, pro-war commentators had predicted that the people of Iraq would greet American soldiers as liberators, and this scene seemed to prove them right. U.S. defense secretary Donald Rumsfeld compared the day to the collapse of the Iron Curtain. "Saddam Hussein is now taking his rightful place alongside Hitler, Stalin, Lenin, Ceauşescu in the pantheon of failed brutal dictators, and the Iraqi people are well on their way to freedom," he declared. Media commentators were also quick to assign iconic significance to the statue's tumble, ranking it alongside the fall of the Berlin Wall, the protesters facing down tanks at Tiananmen Square and other great events caught on TV.

NBC's Tom Brokaw compared the event to "all the statues of Lenin [that] came down all across the Soviet Union."

"Iraqis Celebrate in Baghdad," reported the *Washington Post*.

"Jubilant Iraqis Swarm the Streets of Capital," said the headline in the *New York Times*.

"It was liberation day in Baghdad," proclaimed the *Boston Globe*.

USA Today ran a photo of the event on its front page, accompanied by an interview with Private Ed Chin's sister, Connie. "It's just amazing, we're just so proud of him," she said.

"If you don't have goose bumps now," gushed Fox News anchor David Asman, "you will never have them in your life."[1]

The Clash of Symbolizations

But there was also a "self-conscious and forced quality" to the images, observed the *Boston Globe*. "Whenever the cameras pulled back, they revealed a relatively small crowd at the statue," wrote *Globe* reporters Matthew Gilbert and Suzanne Ryan.[2] A Reuters long-shot photo of Firdos Square showed that it was nearly empty,[3] ringed by U.S. tanks and marines who had moved in to seal off the square before admitting the Iraqis.[4] A BBC photo sequence of the statue's toppling also showed a sparse crowd of approximately 200 people—much smaller than the demonstrations only nine days later, when thousands of

Iraqis took to the streets of Baghdad, calling for U.S.-led forces to leave the city.[5] *Los Angeles Times* reporter John Daniszewski, who was on the scene to witness the statue's fall, caught an aspect of the day's events that the other reporters missed. Most Iraqis were indeed glad to see Saddam go, he wrote, but he spoke near the scene with an Iraqi businessman, who warned that Americans should not be deceived by the images they were seeing.

"A lot of people are angry at America," the businessman said. "Look how many people they killed. Today I saw some people breaking this monument, but there were people—men and women—who stood there and said in Arabic: Screw America, screw Bush. So all this is not a simple situation."[6]

The visual images, of course, are what most people will remember. Most Americans, including the 300,000 soldiers who risked their lives, genuinely believed that Operation Iraqi Freedom was a noble cause and that they were helping make the world a better, safer place for themselves and their loved ones. But it is worth asking whether the toppling of the statue of Saddam was as spontaneous as it was made to appear. If this scene seemed a bit *too* picture-perfect, perhaps there is a reason. Consider, for example, the remarks made by public relations consultant John W. Rendon—who has worked extensively on Iraq-related projects during the past decade on behalf of clients including the Pentagon and the Central Intelligence Agency—on February 29, 1996, before an audience of cadets at the U.S. Air Force Academy.

"I am not a national security strategist or a military tactician," Rendon said. "I am a politician, and a person who uses communication to meet public policy or corporate policy objectives. In fact, I am an information warrior and a perception manager."[7] He reminded the Air Force cadets that when victorious troops rolled into Kuwait City at the end of the first war in the Persian Gulf, they were greeted by hundreds of Kuwaitis waving small American flags. The scene, flashed around the world on television screens, sent the message that U.S. Marines were being welcomed in Kuwait as liberating heroes.

"Did you ever stop to wonder," Rendon asked, "how the people of Kuwait City, after being held hostage for seven long and painful months, were able to get hand-held American, and for that matter, the flags of other coalition countries?" He paused for effect. "Well, you now know the answer. That was one of my jobs then."[8]

Of course, we have no way of knowing whether Rendon or any other PR specialist helped influence the toppling of Saddam Hussein's statue or other specific images that the public saw during the war in Iraq. Public relations firms often do their work behind the scenes, and Rendon—with whom the Pentagon signed a new agreement in February 2002—has been particularly reticent about discussing his work publicly. But his description of himself as a "perception manager" echoes the language of Pentagon planners, who define "perception management" as "actions to convey and (or) deny selected information and indicators to foreign audiences to influence their emotions, motives, and objective reasoning. . . . In various ways, perception management combines truth projection, operations security, cover, and deception, and [psychological operations]."[9]

The paradox of the American war in Iraq, however, is that perception management has been much more successful at "influencing" the "emotions, motives, and objective reasoning" of the American people than it has been at reaching "foreign audiences." When we see footage of Kuwaitis waving American flags or of Iraqis cheering while U.S. Marines topple a statue of Saddam Hussein, it should be understood that those images target U.S. audiences as much, if not more, than the citizens of Kuwait or Iraq. During Operation Iraqi Freedom, American military power easily overwhelmed Iraq's army, but in the crucial battle for worldwide hearts and minds, America lost badly. On March 18, 2003, the Pew Research Center for the People and the Press published a survey showing where world opinion stood as the war with Iraq commenced. Alarming statistics were starting to appear even in countries that were longtime U.S. allies. Since the beginning of 2002, the percentage of people in France who held a favorable view of the United States had dropped from 63 to 31. In Italy, the percentage had fallen from 70 to 34; in Russia, from 61 to 28; in Turkey, from 30 to 12. Even in England, only 48 percent of the population held a favorable view of the United States, down from 75 percent the previous year.[10]

In Iraq itself, moreover, it became obvious within days of the toppling of Saddam Hussein's statue that although the Iraqi people largely welcomed the dictator's downfall, they were not as eager to throw bouquets of flowers at American soldiers as the scene at Firdos Square seemed to suggest. In the holy city of Najaf, a Muslim cleric who was seen as overly friendly to the United States was assassinated by an angry crowd.[11] In Nasiriyah, some 20,000 people rallied to oppose the U.S. military presence on April 15, only six days after the toppling of Saddam's statue. "Yes to freedom, yes to Islam," they chanted. "No to America, no to Saddam."[12] In other protests, crowds chanted "No, no, Chalabi" in opposition to Ahmed Chalabi, the U.S.-backed head of the Iraqi National Congress.[13] *Newsweek* interviewed a high-ranking U.S. military officer who said that he was stunned when he began talking to Iraqis, even anti-Saddam locals, about Chalabi's credibility. "It's astonishing how little support he has," the officer said. "I'm afraid we're backing the wrong horse."[14]

Reality is messy, of course, especially in the aftermath of war, and these developments do not necessarily imply that disaster looms on the horizon as the United States tries to juggle the tension between occupying Iraq militarily and acting as its liberator. They do, however, suggest that the situation is more complicated than the images of victory that looked so unambiguously inspiring on American television. It is important, therefore, that we ask ourselves what lies behind those images, how they have been constructed, and what they may be hiding.

1. Branding America

IN THE AFTERMATH of the terror attacks of September 11, 2001, Americans felt horror, anger and outright astonishment. "I'm amazed that there's such misunderstanding of what our country is about that people would hate us," said President Bush. "We've got to do a better job of making our case."[1] Congressman Tom Lantos struggled to understand why "the white venom of hate is oozing" from countries like Indonesia and Pakistan, "two nations that we have helped enormously since they gained independence."[2] Illinois congressman Henry Hyde wondered why "the popular press overseas, often including the government-owned media, daily depict the United States as a force for evil."[3]

Believing that the answer lay in more "public diplomacy" (a government term for "public relations"),[4] Lantos and Hyde sponsored House Resolution 3969, also known as the *Freedom Promotion Act of 2002*, which instructed the U.S. secretary of state to "make public diplomacy an integral component in the planning and execution of United States foreign policy" and to establish "fully capable multimedia programming and distribution capacity including satellite, Internet, and other services, and also including the capability to acquire and produce audio and video feeds and Internet streaming to foreign news organizations." In addition to sponsoring cultural exchanges and programs to train foreign journalists, the bill set aside $135 million for broadcasting pro-U.S. television programs into the Middle East.[5]

Some of the Bush administration's advice came from Jack Leslie, chairman of Weber Shandwick Worldwide, one of the world's largest public relations firms.[6] Leslie proposed that the United States adopt a PR version of the "Powell doctrine" of using "overwhelming force" as its communications strategy: "No tactic should be ruled out," Leslie said. "CNN ran a segment recently on a pro-bin Laden video game becoming popular in many Islamic countries. Whether we counter with our own video games, use commercial advertising, the Internet, posters or pamphlets—you name it, every tactical approach should be considered that can deliver the right message to the right targets with credibility. . . . If we do these things, if we commit to using overwhelming force with clear objectives and targeting, if we have centralized planning and a chain of command, if we reach out to the best creative minds here and abroad, if we demonstrate a willingness to employ innovative tactics and sound, actionable research then I believe America's message will be heard."[7]

Ten days after September 11, the *Wall Street Journal* reported that the United States was launching two separate advertising campaigns. The first, featuring First Lady Laura Bush, was intended to shore up domestic morale with reassurances that life would go on as it had before the attacks. The second, distributed to networks by the Advertising Council, focused on highlighting the idea that the United States is a racially tolerant nation where people from diverse ethnic and religious backgrounds live in peace.[8]

During the period between 9/11 and the war in Afghanistan, the United States established "instant response" communications offices in Washington, London and Islamabad, Pakistan, with senior administration officials regularly talking to Arabic news media. The *Wall Street Journal* reported that "U.S. officials have scrambled to persuade local editors and broadcasters across South Asia and the Middle East to carry stories intended to soothe anti-American passions and win tolerance for military action. They include features on the importance of Muslims in American life and hard news reports on evidence linking Mr. bin Laden to the attacks." The effort also included "deploying forces to mount psychological operations, or 'psy-ops,' inside

Afghanistan. These forces will be prepared to broadcast messages and distribute leaflets in hopes of dividing the Taliban militia and encouraging a wider anti-Taliban uprising."[9]

That same month, former advertising executive Charlotte Beers was named the State Department's undersecretary of state for public diplomacy. Within the advertising industry, Beers was a legendary figure known as the "queen of Madison Avenue."[10] Prior to her retirement in 2000, she had held the chairman and CEO jobs at two of the world's top ten ad agencies— J. Walter Thompson and Ogilvy & Mather. The *New York Times* reported that she was "planning a television and advertising campaign to try to influence Islamic opinion; one segment could feature American celebrities, including sports stars, and a more emotional message."[11] In an interview with *Advertising Age*, Beers said that public diplomacy "is a vital new arm in what will combat terrorism over time. All of a sudden, we are in this position of redefining who America is, not only for ourselves under this kind of attack, but also for the outside world."[12]

Ad Age reported that Beers was seeking assistance on developing her campaign from the Advertising Council, a nonprofit organization that brings together the government, the media, corporate sponsors and the advertising industry. Originally known as the "War Advertising Council" following the Japanese bombing of Pearl Harbor, the Ad Council has subsequently devised campaigns that encourage people in the United States to vote, use zip codes, participate in the census, and join the National Guard and Reserve. It has introduced familiar icons into the American consciousness including Smokey the Bear, McGruff the Crime Dog and the crash-test dummies, and has added memorable slogans to our vocabulary including "Friends don't let friends drive drunk" and the United Negro College Fund's "A mind is a terrible thing to waste." Its experience in overseas propaganda, however, is limited. In its work with Beers, reported *Ad Age*, the Ad Council "boiled its message down to one strategic idea: freedom."[13]

Voice of America dramatically increased its radio broadcasts in Arabic, Dari, Pashto, Farsi and Urdu,[14] but had difficulty reaching crucial elements of the Arab and Muslim population in the Middle East. "We have almost no youthful audience under the age of 25 in the Arab world and we are concerned that . . . this important segment of the population has enormous distrust of the United States," said Marc Nathanson, a spokesman for the Broadcasting Board of Governors, the entity that oversees international public broadcasting operations for the United States.[15]

Almost from the beginning, in fact, even before bombs started falling on Afghanistan, the U.S. propaganda blitz seemed destined to fail in the Muslim world, for almost the same reasons that the Powell doctrine of "overwhelming force" had been so successful as a military strategy. Bombardments may succeed in destroying or scattering enemy soldiers, but bombardments of rhetoric can annoy and offend their targets. "No amount of media management will matter if the US is not also seen—and actually working on—ways to resolve some of the intractable conflicts which have served to feed fanaticism and anti-US sentiment throughout many Arabic and Islamic nations," said Lee McKnight, director of the Edward R. Murrow Center at Tufts University's Fletcher School of Law and Diplomacy. "We can't convince anyone we're right if we don't understand their point of view," McKnight said.[16]

Contrary to what Henry Hyde and President Bush seemed to believe, there is nothing new in the notion that better marketing will help sell the United States in "countries that hate us." This idea has been tried in the past, and it has largely failed, for many of the same reasons that it has been failing recently. Throughout the latter half of the twentieth century—and recently as well, as we will see shortly when we further examine the legacy of Charlotte Beers—attempts to market the United States as "brand freedom" came into conflict with a U.S. tendency to talk rather than listen, combined with U.S. support of undemocratic regimes whose violent repression contradicted America's stated principles.

That Was Then, This Is Now

The United States first undertook an extensive campaign of propaganda in the Middle East during the Truman and Eisenhower administrations, when the U.S. was expanding efforts to incorporate the region into a global anti-Soviet alliance. In addition to maintaining Western control of oil resources, U.S.

planners were concerned by the rise of Arab nationalism as expressed by the pan-Arabist government of Gamal Abdel Nasser in Egypt and by the sympathy that Arabs expressed toward newly liberated former colonial nations that were frequently pro-Soviet—sympathies that fed anti-Western sentiments and resentment of Israel.

The National Security Archive (NSA), a nonprofit organization that publishes declassified U.S. government documents, has compiled an "electronic briefing book," edited by NSA analyst Joyce Battle, which details many of the early U.S. propaganda activities in the Middle East, beginning in the 1950s. Her report details attempts to influence Arab opinion using methods including books, movies, newsreels, pamphlets, posters, magazines, radio, music, schools, libraries, person-to-person exchanges and religious appeals.[17] A U.S. National Security Council report in 1952 said that aid programs should be designed to achieve "psychological" objectives. The U.S. provided behind-the-scenes funding to magazines in Iran and Iraq, controlling their content and inserting "direct hard-hitting anti-Sov[iet] material."[18] In Iran, the American Embassy planned to disseminate books on contemporary history, political philosophy and fiction, going out of its way to ensure that "publications would bear a publisher's name and have no obvious connection to the Embassy."[19] Walt Disney was approached to see if he "as a patriotic duty could be interested in preparing such a film that could be used to defend democracy."[20] In Iraq, embassy staff even wrote their own cartoon script, featuring a scary bear (symbolizing the Soviet Union) menacing prehistoric humans.[21] Posters disseminated by the U.S. Information Service depicted a "greedy red pig" with a Communist hammer and sickle for a tail.[22]

Even in the 1950s, U.S. propaganda efforts ran into problems with their own contradictions. In Saudi Arabia, the U.S. ambassador noted that U.S. materials had "the double objective of promoting and encouraging democratic government on the one hand while presenting the dangers of communism on the other." However, "since Saudi Arabia is an absolute monarchy its government cannot be expected to welcome propaganda of the first category."[23] The embassy advised against offending the Saudi leadership in order to obtain Saudi cooperation internationally and "protect U.S. oil investment."[24] In other countries as well, efforts to promote U.S.-style democracy were contradicted by the U.S. government's mutually beneficial relationships with repressive regimes.

Sometimes, U.S. support for anti-Communist propaganda actually helped feed the anti-Israel and anti-American sentiments that authoritarian regimes in the region sought to exploit for their own propaganda purposes. In Iraq, the U.S. supported an anti-Communist program focused on schools and universities. The U.S. Information Service helped the Iraqi regime of the day spread the anti-Communist message by alleging "links between Communism and Zionism," reflecting "the feeling of the Director General of Propaganda that this is the best anti-

Communist approach."[25] A memorandum from the U.S. Embassy in Baghdad noted, however, that "Since support for Zionism is also linked in the public mind with the United States any such campaign creates a sort of neutralist 'plague on both your houses' attitude and could stir up increased enmity against the United States at the same time."[26] Anti-Communist students spread the Arab nationalist Ba'athist ideology to military officers, who went on to become the nucleus of the country's dominant political party, led by Saddam Hussein.[27]

The contradiction between rhetoric and reality has remained a pattern throughout several subsequent decades of U.S. involvement in the Middle East. The Shah of Iran came to power in 1953 when a CIA-backed coup overthrew Mohammed Mossadegh, the democratically elected president who wanted to nationalize Iranian oil.[28] In the 1970s, Jimmy Carter declared a renewed American commitment to human rights and condemned Soviet abuses while maintaining U.S. support for the Shah of Iran, notwithstanding the Shah's abysmal human rights record. Under the Carter administration, U.S. arms sales to Iran actually accelerated, while Carter reaffirmed his personal loyalty to the Shah through high-profile state visits, publicly praising Iran as "an island of stability in one of the most troubled areas of the world" and calling the Shah a great leader who had won "the respect and the admiration and love" of his people.[29] Yet, as Amnesty International stated at the time, Iran under the Shah had "the highest rate of death penalties in the world, no valid system of civilian courts and a history of torture which is beyond belief. No country in the world has a worse record in human rights than Iran."[30]

The militarization, corruption and cruelty of the Shah's regime led to a militant Islamic revolution that was virulently anti-American. When Iranian students seized the U.S. Embassy and held 52 members of the embassy staff hostage for more than a year, the reaction in the United States was dramatic. Television and newspapers played up the drama of "America Held Hostage." The slogan "Nuke Iran" appeared on T-shirts and automobile bumper stickers, and people displayed yellow ribbons in symbolic support of the hostages. The Ayatollah Khomeini, Iran's Islamic leader, was demonized in the popular press in much the same way that Saddam Hussein was demonized in the 1990s. Then, as now, the U.S. press and politicians displayed astonishing historical amnesia. If your only source of information was U.S. television, you would have come away thinking that the suffering of the hostages was the worst thing that had ever happened to anyone in Iran and that the United States government had a long and noble history of exemplary conduct in the Middle East. And indeed, that is exactly what many Americans believe to this day.

After several decades of declaring Communism the mother of all evils, the United States in the 1980s began to treat Saddam Hussein's formidable Soviet-supplied army in Iraq as a buffer against Iran's Muslim fundamentalism. Ronald Reagan defeated Jimmy Carter in the 1980 presidential campaign and supported Iraq when it attempted to seize control of the Shatt al Arab waterway at the head of the Persian Gulf, an important channel for the oil exports of both countries.[31] The resulting Iran-Iraq War lasted from 1980 to 1988, costing an estimated one million lives and wreaking enormous economic damage on both countries. When Iran appeared to be winning, Reagan decided to secretly supply Saddam's military, providing tactical military intelligence as well as the technology that Iraq used to build chemical and biological weapons.[32]

Although an enormous number of words have been written about Iraq since the summer of 1992, you can search diligently and find very few recent references in the mainstream media to the thoughts and statements that U.S. policymakers and media pundits made about Iraq during the 1980s while the Iran-Iraq War raged. A December 30, 2002, story by *Washington Post* reporter Michael Dobbs offers one of the rare exceptions. Dobbs reviewed thousands of declassified government documents and reported that "U.S. officials saw Baghdad as a bulwark against militant Shiite extremism and the fall of pro-American states such as Kuwait, Saudi Arabia, and even Jordan—a Middle East version of the 'domino theory' in Southeast Asia. That was enough to turn Hussein into a strategic partner and for U.S. diplomats in Baghdad to routinely refer to Iraqi forces as 'the good guys,' in contrast to the Iranians, who were depicted as 'the bad guys.' . . . The administrations of Ronald Reagan and George H. W. Bush authorized the sale to Iraq of numerous items that had both military and civilian applications, including poisonous chemicals and deadly biological viruses, such as anthrax and bubonic plague."[33]

U.S. support for Iraq continued, moreover, even after U.S. Secretary of State George Schultz received an intelligence briefing from State Department analyst Jonathan T. Howe stating that Iraqi troops were resorting to "almost daily use" of chemical weapons against the Iranians.[34] The Reagan administration was so pleased with Iraq's role in driving back the Iranian hordes that it dispatched Donald H. Rumsfeld to Iraq in 1983 as a special envoy to the Middle East, where he shook Saddam's hand, pledged that the United States would regard "any major reversal of Iraq's fortunes as a strategic defeat for the west," and said that Washington was ready for a full resumption of diplomatic relations.[35]

It would be an oversimplification to say that the Reagan administration expressed no concern at all over Saddam's use of chemical weapons. It *did* express concern. Here's what it said, in a March 5, 1984, State Department news release:

The United States strongly condemns the prohibited use of chemical weapons wherever it occurs.[36]

Of course, a verbal condemnation didn't mean that anything would be *done* about it, such as sanctions or a shift away from America's policy of support for Iraq. Spokesman John Hughes, who delivered the statement, added that the United States "finds the present Iranian regime's intransigent refusal to deviate from its avowed objective of eliminating the legitimate government of neighboring Iraq to be inconsistent with the accepted norms of behavior among nations."[37]

In other words, back when Saddam actually started gassing people, his government was considered "legitimate," and Iran's attempt to achieve what the current Bush administration has called "regime change" was "inconsistent with the accepted norms of behavior."

Similar statements came from leading U.S. newspapers. "Privately, some officials were less harsh on the Iraqis," noted the *Washington Post* report on the Reagan administration's March 5 news release. The *Post* added that it was "not surprising" that Iraq would use gas, given the ferocity of their Iranian enemy. A few days later, the *Post* editorialized that it would be "arbitrariness" to "sanction one form of warfare and not another." By year's end, the United States had gone ahead and established full diplomatic relations with Iraq for the first time since 1967. The *Post* heralded the administration's pro-Iraq tilt by saying that Washington was "coming into a better position to play a useful regional role" in the Middle East. In response to reports that Iraq was continuing to use chemical weapons, the *Post* philosophized that it was "a bit odd when you consider all the ways that people have devised to do violence to each other, to worry overly about any particular method."[38]

In 1988, reports emerged that Saddam Hussein had used chemical weapons against his own citizens—Iraqi Kurds in the town of Halabja. Several U.S. senators, including Claiborne Pell

(D–Rhode Island), Al Gore (D–Tennessee) and Jesse Helms (R–North Carolina), introduced the *Prevention of Genocide Act of 1988*, which sought to impose sanctions against Iraq for its continuing use of chemical weapons and for other human rights violations. The act passed in the Senate unanimously, but the Reagan White House launched a campaign to turn it back and succeeded in killing the bill with the help of its allies in the House of Representatives.[39] It is worth noting the role that members of the current Bush administration played in killing the legislation. Former ambassador Peter Galbraith, who served as an Iraq expert for the Senate, recalls that "Secretary of State Colin Powell was then the national security advisor who orchestrated Ronald Reagan's decision to give Hussein a pass for gassing the Kurds. Dick Cheney, then a prominent Republican congressman and now vice president and the Bush administration's leading Iraq hawk, could have helped push the sanctions legislation but did not."[40] In the fall of 1989, only nine months before Iraq's invasion of Kuwait, then-president Bush overrode the objections of officials in three different government agencies and signed a top-secret directive ordering closer ties with Baghdad and opening the way for $1 billion in new aid.[41]

Thanks for the Memories

As a general rule of history, victims have much longer memories of injustice than the people who perpetrate their suffering.

F. Scott Fitzgerald captured this quite elegantly in *The Great Gatsby*: "They were careless people, Tom and Daisy," he wrote. "They smashed up things and creatures and then retreated back to their money or their vast carelessness or whatever it was that kept them together, and let other people clean up the mess they made."

Much the same thing can be said about the people who are responsible for the disastrous course of U.S. foreign policy in the Middle East. On March 16, 2003, just days before the U.S. invasion of Iraq, the *Washington Post* reported that the United States and France were the source in the 1980s for "all the foreign germ samples . . . used to create the biological weapons that are still believed to be in Iraq's arsenal, according to American officials and foreign diplomats who have reviewed Iraq's latest weapons declaration to the United Nations." Naturally, the revelation of this bombshell did not come from any of those officials or diplomats themselves. The bioweapons declaration was obtained by Gary B. Pitts, a Houston attorney representing veterans of Operation Desert Storm. Pitts's clients suffer from Gulf War Syndrome and believe that their illnesses may have been caused by exposure to chemical or biological weapons from Iraq's arsenal.

The government officials and biological supply houses that provided Saddam with anthrax and other germ samples seemed to have few regrets. "They were sent for legitimate research purposes," said Nancy J. Wysocki, vice president for human resources and public relations at the American Type Culture

Collection, a nonprofit scientific resource center that serves as a clearinghouse for the storage and distribution of microorganisms and other biological products. A former U.S. weapons inspector added that the 1980s "were a more innocent time"—a use of "innocent" that perhaps belongs in our chapter on doublespeak.[42]

When asked about the period, Secretary of Defense Donald Rumsfeld develops a remarkably hazy memory. During a hearing on September 19, 2002, U.S. senator Robert Byrd asked Rumsfeld directly, "Did the United States help Iraq to acquire the building blocks of biological weapons during the Iran-Iraq War?"

"Certainly not to my knowledge," Rumsfeld replied.

Byrd read a passage from *Newsweek* in which the U.S. role was detailed.

"I have never heard anything like what you've read," Rumsfeld responded. "I have no knowledge of it whatsoever, and I doubt it."[43]

Two days later, CNN reporter Jamie McIntyre raised the topic again. This time, he had video footage on hand that seemed to take Rumsfeld off guard. "Let me take you back to about 20 years ago," McIntyre began. "The date, I believe, was December 20, 1983. You were meeting with Saddam Hussein, I think we have some video of that meeting. Tell me what was going on during this meeting."

"Where did you get this video," Rumsfeld responded, "from the Iraqi television?"

"We dug this out of the CNN library," McIntyre replied.

"I see," Rumsfeld said. "Isn't that interesting. There I am."
Pressed further, Rumsfeld suddenly *did* manage to remember
a detail, saying, "I cautioned him about the use of chemical
weapons, as a matter of fact."[44] There is no record of any such
warning in any official documents or other record from Rumsfeld's trip.[45]

Unfortunately, those who cannot remember the past tend to
repeat it, which explains why U.S. officials continue to repeat
the propaganda strategies of the 1950s. Rather than changing
the way we actually *relate* to the people of the Middle East, they
still dream of fixing their image through some new marketing
campaign cooked up in Hollywood or on Madison Avenue.

Beers for America

In announcing that he was putting Charlotte Beers in charge of
reversing America's image as the Great Satan of the Islamic
world, Secretary of State Colin Powell explained that "it was an
attempt to change from just selling the U.S. . . . to really branding foreign policy."[46] Beers had made her name in the private
sector selling Uncle Ben's rice and Head & Shoulders shampoo
before going to work for some of the world's leading advertising
agencies.[47] Powell had met her previously in the 1990s when
both served on the board of Gulfstream Aerospace. "Guess
what? She got *me* to buy Uncle Ben's Rice," Powell reasoned.

"So there is nothing wrong with getting somebody who knows how to sell something."[48]

Beers brought to the job the same attitudes and skills that she used as a commercial advertiser. One of her first thoughts was to find "a great athlete, celebrity or singer" to sell America, which she characterized as an "elegant brand."[49] Her frequent use of the word "branding" reflected her reputation as a specialist in brand management, which the *Washington Post* described as "a quasi-alchemical process that promises to identify a particular company's product with desirable attributes like 'taste' or 'quality.'" As Beers herself explained it, "You'll find that in any great brand, the leverageable asset is the emotional underpinning of the brand."[50]

Muslim sports figures considered to be good candidates to endorse America included Muhammad Ali and NBA star Hakeem Olajuwon.[51] During the war in Afghanistan, Beers oversaw the design of posters to promote a "Reward for Justice" program that offered millions of dollars for information leading to the capture of Osama bin Laden. Another initiative, called "Can a Woman Stop Terrorism?" attempted to tell "the stories of women who have come forward and aided in the capture of terrorists." She also oversaw the creation of "Muslim Life in America," which depicted, via a website and glossy color brochures in multiple languages, the tolerance and respect that Muslims experience in the United States.[52] As the new moon ushered in the month of Ramadan in November 2001, U.S. officials prepared "Mosques of America" posters, showing glossy images of domes and minarets, for distribution across the Arab world. President Bush and ambassadors in the Middle East and Asia welcomed Muslims into their homes to mark *iftar*, or the breaking of the fast. According to a senior State Department official, "We are demonstrating to the Muslim world that Americans take [Muslim] holidays as seriously as they do Christian and Jewish holidays."[53]

These activities, however, did little to persuade most Muslims, who found the war in Afghanistan more disturbing than anything that handshakes or posters could address. The irony is that of all the military activities in which the United States has engaged during the past 50 years, the war in Afghanistan was certainly one of the easiest to defend on its merits. The terrorism of 9/11 had provoked the U.S. well beyond the point at which any nation capable of responding militarily would feel compelled to do so. Moreover, the Taliban that ruled Afghanistan not only harbored Osama bin Laden but had a record of such brutality that a war to drive them from power would likely save more lives than it would cost. Nevertheless, much of the Muslim world reacted to the war with mistrust, and the Beers communication strategy did not even attempt to justify it. The most frequent issues raising alarm in the Arab world were U.S. support for Israel, U.S. backing of authoritarian regimes such as those in Saudi Arabia and Egypt, and America's reputation as a bullying superpower. The Beers branding strategy offered feel-good imagery but avoided those key issues entirely.

"Even in Britain, America's most reliable ally, support for

war has fallen from around three-quarters to two-thirds, despite the hyperactivity of Tony Blair, the British prime minister, who has traveled thousands of miles in the past few weeks putting the case for the war," reported the *Economist*. "Some polls say four out of ten British Muslims think al-Qaeda's attacks are in some way justified; a handful have actually volunteered to fight with the Taliban. In France, support has dropped from two-thirds to half. In both Germany and Italy, well over half the population wants the attacks on Afghanistan to end."

In the Middle East itself, of course, things were worse, as the United States found that it had no reservoir of trust on which it could draw. "Unlike in Europe, where opinion has been changing only recently, Arab opinion hardened early on," the *Economist* reported. "But the passage of time has led to a subtle and worrying development. The burden of proof has shifted: America is being asked to prove it is not waging war against Islam."[54] The relative ease with which U.S. troops routed the Taliban on the battlefield made no difference; on the battlefield of world public opinion, the United States lost badly.

In January 2002, Beers spent three days in Cairo, Egypt, talking about mending fences as part of her "Dialogue with Islam" campaign. She seemed to be having a little trouble, however, with the "listening" part of the dialogue equation. "Egyptians who spoke with her came away shaking their heads," the *New York Times* reported, "saying American officials do not appreciate that Muslims feel picked on by the United States, or how deep feelings run for the Palestinian cause—or just how heavily history weighs here."[55]

"The United States says that U.N. resolutions should be applied everywhere in the world except Israel. Why?" asked Egyptian newspaper editor Muhammad Abdel Hadi. He complained that American officials brush him off when he makes this point. "They say, 'Forget about the past, let's talk about the moment.' . . . Every American political speech is the same," he said. "Ms. Beers expressed herself like President Bush in every possible way. No matter how hard you try to make them understand, they don't."[56]

In fact, the *New York Times* reported that "the Afghan conflict seems to have confirmed Osama bin Laden as a folk hero." According to an Egyptian merchant interviewed by the *Times*, "Anyone who is a Muslim who says 'No' to the United States is a hero. Every day you turn on the television and you see the Israelis killing Palestinians with U.S. weapons. No matter how much the U.S. tries to change its image in the Arab world, what we are seeing with our own eyes is much stronger." According to a Saudi Arabian commentator, every scene of dead civilians in Afghanistan serves as a recruitment tool for anti-Americanism. "The whole Muslim world is watching this with shock and horror," he said. "Among the young, new animosities are created and there are new calls for revenge. This is dangerous; this is the atmosphere that creates terrorism, creates extremism."[57]

On April 24, 2002, Beers testified before Congress. "In late

February, Gallup released its poll of almost 10,000 people in nine predominantly Muslim countries, and found that by a margin of two to one, residents of these nations had an unfavorable opinion of the U.S.," she said. "Some of the specific results of the poll were not surprising in places like Iran, but in Kuwait for instance only 28% of those residents polled had a favorable opinion of the U.S. This, in a country that was liberated by the U.S. and our allies only a decade ago. In Morocco the favorable number was only 22%, and in Saudi Arabia, one of our strongest allies in the region, only 18% expressed a favorable opinion of the U.S."[58]

Beers asked Congress for $595 million to "improve and magnify the ways in which we are addressing people of the world." Much of the money would be spent on opinion polling "in Muslim countries and communities to provide policymakers with information on foreign publics' attitudes, perceptions, and opinions so public diplomacy messages can be more effectively targeted," Beers said. In addition to "regular polls in Afghanistan and in Muslim-majority countries," she proposed increased polling in Africa, Indonesia, Thailand, the Philippines, Europe, Latin America, Russia and the former Soviet republics. Yet notwithstanding all the money being planned for "listening" activities, there was little evidence that the U.S. had heard or was prepared to respond in a substantive way to any of the strongly expressed opinions coming from the Arab world.

In October 2002, while the Bush administration used the push for war with Iraq as the centerpiece of its midterm election strategy, Beers launched her latest initiative—a $5 million "Shared Values" advertising campaign, designed by the McCann-Erickson marketing firm. Dubbed a "Muslim-as-Apple-Pie" campaign by the *New York Times*, the "Shared Values" videos featured photogenic Muslim-Americans playing with their children and going about their jobs. One TV commercial showed Rawia Ismail, a Lebanese-born schoolteacher who now lives in Toledo, Ohio. Her head covered with an Islamic scarf, Ismail was shown with her smiling children in her all-American kitchen, at a school softball game and extolling American values as she taught her class. "I didn't see any prejudice anywhere in my neighborhood after September 11," she said.[59]

The problem with these messages is not that they were necessarily false. The problem is that, like the rest of the Beers campaign, "Shared Values" avoided discussing the issues at the core of Muslim resentment of the United States—the Palestinian-Israeli conflict and the history of U.S. intervention in the region. "We know that there's religious freedom in America, and we like that. What we're angry about is the arrogant behavior of the U.S. in the rest of the world," said Ahmad Imron, an economics student in Indonesia, after watching one of the "Shared Values" TV ads.[60]

Beers also launched "Next Chapter," a TV show broadcast by Voice of America via satellite to Iran. Described by the *New York Times* as a "hip" and "MTV-style" show about youth culture, "Next Chapter" aimed at winning the hearts and minds of young people.[61] She launched Radio Sawa, a station that broadcasts pop music in the Arab world, accompanied by top-of-the-hour news from an American point of view.[62] She sponsored a worldwide traveling exhibition of photographs of the ravaged World Trade Center site. Another Beers project recruited prominent American writers, inviting them to contribute to an anthology of essays on "what it means to be an American writer" and to give readings around the globe in a campaign intended to promote international appreciation of American culture.[63] One of the authors asked to travel abroad was former CIA analyst Ken Pollack, author of *The Threatening Storm: The Case for Invading Iraq.* Beers explained his recruitment as an effort to achieve "third party authenticity . . . we desperately need to have other voices speaking for us. . . . He's that third voice."[64]

In another effort to achieve "third party authenticity," a group called the Council of American Muslims for Understanding (CAMU) launched its own website, called Open Dialogue. "It will be government-funded, but it's not government-founded. I'd like to say we founded it," said the group's chairman, Malik Hasan, who nonetheless admitted that the idea for CAMU began with the State Department.[65] Visitors to the website, whose declared mission was "bringing people and cultures together through dialogue," were invited to send away for a free copy of "Muslim Life in America," to view the stories of Rawia Ismail and the others profiled in the "Shared Values" TV commercials, or to "tell us your story" by sending an e-mail.[66]

The striking thing about the CAMU website, however, is

how *little* real dialogue it enabled. This is, after all, the twenty-first century. Internet newsgroups, web forums, e-mail listservs and even webcams have long ago perfected the technologies that enable real dialogue to occur in real time between people throughout the world. The absence of opportunities for genuine dialogue may explain why Open Dialogue has been irrelevant to most people seeking information about U.S.-Muslim relations. A Google search on April 8, 2003, found only 58 other web pages that link to Open Dialogue, most of which were sites run by U.S. embassies or other government agencies. For comparison's sake, there were 2,200 links to IslamiCity.com, a site that discusses world affairs from a Muslim point of view.

As author Naomi Klein observed not long after Beers began working for the State Department, the U.S. refusal to genuinely engage with its "target audience" was linked to her "branding" strategy. "In the corporate world," Klein wrote, "once a 'brand identity' is settled upon, it is enforced with military precision throughout a company's operations. . . . At its core, branding is about rigorously controlled one-way messages, sent out in their glossiest form, then sealed off from those who would turn corporate monologue into social dialogue." This approach may work for corporations but not for governments. "When companies try to implement global image consistency, they look like generic franchises. But when governments do the same, they can look distinctly authoritarian," Klein wrote. "It's no coincidence that the political leaders most preoccupied with branding themselves and their parties were also allergic to democracy and diversity. Historically, this has been the ugly flipside of politicians striving for consistency of brand: centralised information, state-controlled media, re-education camps, purging of dissidents and much worse."[67]

By any measure, the Beers strategy was an abject failure. A poll released in December 2002 by the Pew Research Center found steep declines in America's public image in every Muslim country surveyed. In Egypt (typically the second-largest recipient of U.S. government aid), only 6 percent of respondents said that they had a "favorable" view of the United States.[68] In a speech that month to the National Press Club, Beers admitted the difficulty that she was having in penetrating the Middle Eastern media. "We only have one choice in the world of the Middle East and Southeast. We have to buy the media itself," she said.[69] But even paying wasn't working. Less than a month after the launch of the "Shared Values" advertising campaign, the State Department abruptly suspended it. The TV ads were controversial in the countries where they aired, and government-run channels in Egypt, Lebanon and Jordan flatly refused to run them at all. "Islamic opinion is influenced more by what the U.S. does than by anything it can say," commented an advertising executive in the *Wall Street Journal*.[70]

On March 3, 2003, barely two weeks before the U.S. attack on Iraq, Beers resigned for unspecified "health reasons."[71] Her resignation marked the low point of her career and was heralded with jeers by some of the same marketing industry colleagues who had previously praised her genius. The editor of

O'Dwyer's PR Daily described her work as "botched propaganda efforts" that "failed miserably."[72] But in fairness to a woman who was seen as a brilliant star in the corporate advertising community until she landed the "America account," it should be noted that Beers followed a strategy similar to the advice that came from other PR and marketing executives following September 11. Carl Weiser, a Washington correspondent for the Gannett News Service, interviewed a number of them to ask what kind of campaign they would create to convince the Islamic world "that this nation is not the Great Satan, but good and generous." Most of their responses focused on cosmetic concerns rather than real issues. One consultant thought that American tourists need to behave more politely when traveling abroad. Jack Bergen, president of the Council of Public Relations Firms, suggested bringing journalists, editors and columnists from the Arab world to the United States so they could appreciate us better. According to Los Angeles marketing consultant Rob Frankel, "This is a branding issue, plain and simple. . . . Countries are no different than soap flakes or automobiles." In branding terms, he said, "we should be the gentle giant, not the menacing ogre. Or in corporate terms, we should be Federal Express, not Microsoft."[73]

These ideas are not just shallow and superficial. They are wrong. They do not even begin to address the serious issues that have driven a wedge between the United States and Muslims throughout the world. The main problem, Arabs would tell you, was not how Charlotte Beers handled her task but the product she was selling. From the outset, in fact, her failure was predicted by observers such as Osama Siblani, publisher of the *Arab American News*. "The United States lost the public relations war in the Muslim world a long time ago," Siblani said in October 2001. "They could have the prophet Muhammad doing public relations and it wouldn't help."[74]

2. War Is Sell

"**FROM A MARKETING POINT** of view, you don't introduce new products in August," White House chief of staff Andrew H. Card, Jr., told the *New York Times* in September 2002. Card was explaining what the *Times* characterized as a "meticulously planned strategy to persuade the public, the Congress, and the allies of the need to confront the threat from Saddam Hussein."[1]

According to the article, intensive planning for the "Iraq roll-out" had begun in July. Bush advisers checked the congressional calendar for the best time to launch a "full-scale lobbying campaign." The effort started the day after Labor Day as Congress reconvened and congressional leaders received invitations to the White House and the Pentagon for Iraq briefings with Vice President Dick Cheney, Secretary of Defense Donald Rumsfeld and CIA director George Tenet. White House communications aides scouted locations for the president's September 11, 2002, address and chose Ellis Island, with the Statue of Liberty as a backdrop. The following day, Bush appeared before the United Nations to ask for a security council resolution that would give him the international mandate he needed for war. It was no accident, of course, that the Iraq rollout was timed to coincide with the first anniversary of Al Qaeda's attack on the United States.

The *Washington Post* reported that the White House had created an Office of Global Communications (OGC) to "coordinate the administration's foreign policy message and supervise America's image abroad."[2] In September, the *Times* of London reported that the OGC would spend $200 million for a "PR blitz against Saddam Hussein" aimed "at American and foreign audiences, particularly in Arab nations skeptical of US policy in the region." The campaign would use "advertising techniques to persuade crucial target groups that the Iraqi leader must be ousted."[3]

"We're getting the band together," said White House communications director Dan Bartlett in September 2002. The "band," explained *Newsweek*'s Martha Brant, refers to "the people who brought you the war in Afghanistan—or at least the accompanying public-relations campaign. . . . Now they're back for a reunion tour on Iraq."[4] A group of young White House up-and-comers, the "band" was meeting daily on a morning conference call to plan media strategy with the aim of controlling "the message within the administration so no one—not even Vice President Dick Cheney—freelances on Iraq," Brant wrote. Its main players were Bartlett, Office of Global Communications director Tucker Eskew, and James Wilkinson, a former deputy communications director who was subsequently reassigned to serve as spokesperson to General Tommy Franks at U.S. Central Command in Qatar. Other frequent participants in the planning sessions included top Pentagon spokesperson Victoria ("Torie") Clarke, Cheney adviser Mary Matalin, and Secretary of State Colin Powell's spokesman, Richard Boucher.

PR Week, one of the leading trade publications for the public relations industry, reported that U.S. secretary of defense Donald H. Rumsfeld also relied on an informal "strategic communications" group of beltway lobbyists, PR people and Republican insiders to hone the Pentagon's message. Clarke, who previously ran the Washington office of the Hill & Knowlton PR firm, was reported to have assembled the Rumsfeld group, whose members included Republican PR executive and lobbyist Sheila Tate, beltway lobbyists Charlie Black and Tommy Boggs (also a lobbyist for Saudi Arabia), and Republican spokesman turned columnist Rich Galen. Participants "intermittently offer messaging advice to the Pentagon," reported *PR*

Week. One of the Rumsfeld group's projects was linking the anti-terrorism cause with efforts to convince the public "of the need to engage 'rogue states'—including Iraq—that are likely to harbor terrorists."[5]

Serious Doubts

At the time that the Bush administration's public push for war began, domestic and international support was far from assured. With Muslims resentful of recent U.S. military actions in Afghanistan, voices from many quarters warned that the U.S. reputation had begun to slip worldwide. "Faced with a survey by diplomats showing widespread foreign skepticism about their motives," reported UPI correspondent Eli Lake, the United States was "planning a public relations offensive to build international support among foreign opinion leaders for a war against Iraq." For starters, the Iraq Public Diplomacy Group, "which includes representatives from the CIA, National Security Council, Pentagon, State Department and the U.S. Agency for International Development," planned to publish a brochure and hold interactive teleconferences targeting "opinion leaders" in Europe and the Middle East.[6]

The congressional election–season timing of the campaign prompted some observers to wonder if the Bush administration was really serious or if it was merely using war talk to distract attention from economic issues such as the recession and the

Enron scandal. "If nothing else, the Bush administration has succeeded in making 'Should we attack Iraq?' the most-considered
political question in the US today," observed *PR Week*. Other
questions had been pushed to the background, *PR Week* added,
such as "How do we punish corporate criminals?" "How do we
balance civil liberties with national security?" "Where is Osama
bin Laden?" and "What about the economy?"[7]

Similar observations came from Jack Leslie, chairman of
Weber Shandwick Worldwide, one of the world's largest PR
firms. "Better this than a lot of domestic issues that could be at
the forefront," said Leslie, who has served as a consultant to the
White House since September 11. "Not to suggest that this is
all [a diversion], but surely they would rather have a debate
around Iraq than other issues."[8]

"Senior Republican Party officials say the prospect of at least
two more weeks of Congressional debate on Iraq is allowing
their party to run out the clock on the fall election, blocking
Democrats as they try to seize on the faltering economy and
other domestic concerns as campaign issues," reported the *New
York Times* on September 20, 2002. "A striking reminder of how
the war talk has drowned out issues that Democrats believe
work in their favor came on Thursday, when the Dow Jones average sunk to 7,940. That was the lowest it had been since last
July, when many Democrats believed that the nation's fixation
on a plummeting market and reports of corporate malfeasance
were setting the stage for Democrats to win control of both
houses of Congress. Asked today if the latest dip on Wall Street

drew the kind of coverage the last one did, a senior Democratic strategist responded with a glum e-mail message: 'Not at all. War, war, war.'"[9]

For prominent figures within the Bush administration, however, war with Iraq was not merely election-season chatter. It came as the consummation of plans and discussions that began more than ten years earlier, shortly after the end of the first U.S.-led war in the Persian Gulf.

The "George Washington of Iraq"

In 1991, a few months after the end of Operation Desert Storm, then-president George H. W. Bush signed a presidential directive ordering a CIA covert operation to unseat Saddam Hussein. In turn, the CIA hired public relations consultant John W. Rendon to organize anti-Saddam propaganda campaigns inside Iraq.

Rendon is a former election campaign consultant to Democratic Party politicians, including Michael Dukakis and Jimmy Carter. His PR firm, the Rendon Group, now specializes in assisting U.S. military operations. In addition to Iraq, the Rendon Group has worked in Argentina, Colombia, Haiti, Kosovo, Panama and Zimbabwe. Rendon first began working in Iraq during the buildup to Desert Storm, when he received $100,000 per month for media work on behalf of the Kuwaiti royal family.[10] (His success at persuading liberated Kuwaitis to wave

American flags was mentioned in the introduction to this book.) During the first year of Rendon's post-war contract with the CIA, the PR firm spent more than $23 million producing videos and comic books ridiculing Saddam, a traveling photo exhibit of Iraqi atrocities and two separate radio programs that broadcast messages from Kuwait into Iraq, mocking the regime and calling on Iraqi army officers to defect.[11]

In what may have been the Rendon Group's most significant project, in 1992 it helped organize the Iraqi National Congress (INC), which represented the first major attempt by opponents of Saddam Hussein to join forces.[12] According to a February 1998 ABC News report by Peter Jennings, Rendon came up with the name for the INC and channeled $12 million of covert CIA funding to it between 1992 and 1996.[13] The INC brought together Kurds and Arabs, Sunnis and Shiites, secularists and Islamists, liberal democrats, old-style nationalists and ex–military officers. In October 1992, Ahmed Chalabi, a Rendon protégé, was appointed to head the group.

Chalabi has what can safely be called a "colorful past." Born in Baghdad in 1945, he was the son of a wealthy Shiite family with close ties to the monarchy that was installed in Iraq by Lawrence of Arabia after the First World War. At age 13, Chalabi was forced to flee the country with his family when the monarchy was toppled in a coup led by Abdul-Karim Qassem. (Four years later, Qassem's assassination would bring the Ba'ath party to power, paving the way for the rise of Saddam Hussein.) Chalabi grew up in Jordon, Lebanon, England and the United

States, attending MIT and the University of Chicago, and teaching math at the American University of Beirut before establishing the Petra Bank in 1977, which came to be the second-largest commercial bank in Jordan. His career as a banker lasted for 12 years until 1989, when, in an episode still surrounded by controversy, the government of Jordan seized the bank and pumped in $164 million to save it from financial collapse. Chalabi fled the country and was tried in absentia and sentenced to 22 years of hard labor for embezzlement, fraud and currency-trading irregularities. According to Jordan's version of events, he had successfully absconded with more than $70 million.[14]

Chalabi himself tells the story differently, claiming that the government of Jordan cracked down for political reasons, to stop him from funding Saddam Hussein's opponents inside Iraq. It's possible that this is true, since by that time Chalabi was already active in anti-Iraq opposition groups and had a connection with Richard Perle, an assistant defense secretary in the Reagan administration whose intrigues in the Middle East are numerous and have continued under the current Bush administration. "Of course, the fact that Chalabi may have been prosecuted for political reasons does not mean that he is innocent of embezzlement and fraud," observes reporter Robert Dreyfuss, who profiled Chalabi for The *American Prospect* in November 2002. "In any case, allegations of self-dealing have followed him everywhere since."[15]

Under Chalabi's leadership, the INC attempted to develop a paramilitary presence inside Iraq with the stated goal of creating a provisional government and launching attacks on Iraqi cities. In a pattern that has continued to mark his leadership of the INC, however, he quickly fell out with a number of his supporters. According to Laith Kubba, a former INC spokesman, "His priorities were on lobbying Washington rather than to reach out to Iraqis, develop policy papers or work out what should be the national agenda."[16] Internal differences led to the group's virtual collapse, and for years afterward, Chalabi was mistrusted by the CIA and the Clinton administration, which dropped the INC and began funding a rival opposition group, the Iraqi National Accord (INA). That venture also ended disastrously, when a number of INC and INA members were rounded up and killed by Saddam Hussein's forces.[17]

By this time, a good portion of the U.S. intelligence and military establishment had decided that the INC was a waste of time. General Anthony, who was commanding officer of the U.S. Central Command under President Clinton, referred sarcastically to the INC's planned military incursion into Iraq as a "Bay of Goats" operation dreamed up by "some silk-suited, Rolex-wearing guys in London."[18] A CIA financial audit in the mid-1990s found that Chalabi had engaged in sloppy accounting with U.S. taxpayers' money.[19] Nevertheless, he remained a frequent visitor to the corridors of power in Washington. Certain circles—the pro-Israel hawks with roots in the Reagan and first Bush administrations who have come to be known as "neoconservatives"—even referred to Chalabi as the "George Washington of Iraq."[20] And Chalabi knew how to tell them what they wanted to hear, promising that Saddam's regime was on its last legs, that the INC commanded vast sympathetic support and intelligence assets, and that mass defections of Iraqi forces would happen as soon as the U.S. showed the gumption to support a war of liberation.

Chronicle of a War Foretold

Chalabi's political fortunes improved in 1997, when a number of prominent neoconservatives formed the Project for the New American Century (PNAC), which lobbied for increasing U.S. military spending and taking a harder line against Iraq.[21] PNAC's founder and chairman, William Kristol, was a former chief of staff to Vice President Dan Quayle and to Secretary of Education William Bennett (both PNAC founding members themselves). Kristol was better known as the editor of the *Weekly Standard*, an influential political affairs magazine underwritten by right-wing media mogul Rupert Murdoch. Many of the other PNAC founders would later hold important positions within the second Bush administration. Members included:

- Elliott Abrams, a former Reagan-era assistant secretary of state for inter-American affairs. During the Iran-Contra scandal, Abrams pleaded guilty to two misdemeanor counts of lying to Congress but was later pardoned by the first Bush administration. He later became president of the Ethics in Public Policy Center and was subsequently appointed as a member of George W. Bush's National Security Council.

- Jeb Bush, the governor of Florida and the president's brother.
- Vice President Dick Cheney.
- Retired Generals Wayne Downing, Buster Glosson, and Barry McCaffrey (who also served as the Clinton administration's drug czar).
- Steve Forbes, publisher, billionaire, and Republican presidential candidate in 1996 and 2000.
- Francis Fukuyama, author of *The End of History and the Last Man*, a popular book of the 1990s that claimed that the fall of Communism marked "the end of history as such: that is, the end point of mankind's ideological evolution and the universalization of Western liberal democracy as the final form of human government."
- Former House speaker Newt Gingrich.
- Bruce P. Jackson, a former vice president at Lockheed Martin, who also previously served as an aide to former Secretaries of Defense Frank Carlucci and Dick Cheney.
- Robert Kagan, former secretary of state George Shultz's speechwriter under President Reagan.
- Jeane Kirkpatrick, a White House and Pentagon adviser under former presidents Reagan and Bush.
- Lewis Libby, Cheney's chief of staff.

* Top Pentagon adviser Richard Perle, who helped sell the 1991 war in the Persian Gulf as co-chair of the Committee for Peace and Security in the Gulf (CPSG).

* Norman Podhoretz, the longtime editor of *Commentary* magazine, which frequently features policy articles by officials from conservative U.S. presidential administrations.

* Secretary of Defense Donald Rumsfeld.

* Paul Wolfowitz, Rumsfeld's deputy.

* Former CIA director turned lobbyist James Woolsey, whose law firm, Shea & Gardner, has represented the Iraqi National Congress.[22]

In 1998, PNAC lobbied for Congress to approve the 1998 *Iraqi Liberation Act*, which made "regime change" an official U.S. policy and authorized $97 million in aid for Iraqi opposition groups including the INC. In testimony before Congress on February 25, 1998, Paul Wolfowitz urged Congress to authorize the bill as a way of getting rid of Saddam without using U.S. ground troops. "Help the Iraqi people remove him from power," Wolfowitz said. He added, "However—and I think this is very important—the estimate that it would take a major invasion with U.S. ground forces seriously overestimates Saddam Hussein."[23]

At the time, these words were intended to reassure members of Congress. The idea of U.S.-engineered "regime change" was still considered radical and dangerous, and Wolfowitz wanted to make it clear that he was not asking them to sign on to the even more dangerous idea of drawing America into an outright war. Five years later, however, the inauguration of George W. Bush and the post-9/11 war on terrorism would put Wolfowitz and other neoconservatives back in the driver's seat of U.S. foreign policy. Nine days after the September 11 attacks, PNAC sent an open letter to President Bush, calling not only for the destruction of Osama bin Laden's Al Qaeda network, but also to extend the war to Iraq, and to take measures against Iran, Syria, Lebanon and the Palestinian Authority.[24]

The Information War

The war on terror also meant new work for the Rendon Group. In October 2001, newspapers reported that the Pentagon had awarded Rendon a four-month, $397,000 contract to handle PR aspects of the U.S. military strikes in Afghanistan.[25] In February 2002, about the time that the Afghanistan contract expired, the *New York Times* reported that the Pentagon was using the Rendon Group to assist its new propaganda agency, the Office of Strategic Influence (OSI). The OSI was formally disbanded following a public backlash after the *Times* reported that it would provide foreign reporters with "news items, possibly even false ones."[26] However, Rendon's contract with the Pentagon was not cancelled. Newspapers attempted to interview employees at the Rendon Group about the nature of their work, but they were rebuffed. "Let me just say that we have a confidentiality/nondisclosure agreement in place" with the Department of Defense, said Rendon spokeswoman Jeanne Sklarz.[27]

Rendon's refusal to discuss his activities makes it difficult to do more than speculate about the full scope and extent of his firm's involvement in Iraq, but an incident during the war itself provided a rare breach in the wall of secrecy. On March 23, 2003, TV cameraman Paul Moran was killed in northern Iraq by a suicide bomber while on assignment for the Australian Broadcasting Corporation. His obituary, published in his home town of Adelaide, Australia, noted that Moran's activities "included working for an American public relations company contracted by the U.S. Central Intelligence Agency to run propaganda campaigns against the dictatorship. . . . Company founder John Rendon flew from the U.S. to attend Mr. Moran's funeral in Adelaide on Wednesday. A close friend, Rob Buchan, said that the presence of Mr. Rendon—an adviser to the U.S. National Security Council—illustrated the regard in which Mr. Moran was held in U.S. political circles, including the Congress."[28]

In March 2002, Seymour Hersh reported in the *New Yorker* that groups supported by the Iraqi National Congress "have been conducting sabotage operations inside Iraq, targeting oil refineries and other installations. The latest attack took place on January 23rd, an INC official told me, when missiles fired by what he termed 'indigenous dissidents' struck the large Baiji refinery complex, north of Baghdad, triggering a fire that blazed for more than twelve hours." However, Hersh added, "A dispute over Chalabi's potential usefulness preoccupies the bureaucracy." On the one side, "the civilian leadership in the Pentagon continues to insist that only the INC can lead the opposition." On the other, "the INC's critics note that Chalabi, despite years of effort and millions of dollars in American aid, is intensely unpopular today among many elements in Iraq."[29]

Notwithstanding these concerns, Hersh added that "INC supporters in and around the Administration, including Paul Wolfowitz and Richard Perle, believe, like Chalabi, that any show of force would immediately trigger a revolt against Saddam within Iraq, and that it would quickly expand."[30] Wolfowitz and Perle liked Chalabi in part because he was one of the few members of the Iraqi opposition who shared their future vision for Iraq. In September 2002, *Intelligence Online*, an international newsletter for diplomats, politicians and business executives, reported that there was "a clear split" between Chalabi's INC and the other main opposition group, the Supreme Council for Islamic Revolution in Iraq (SCIRI). The two groups differed over "how Iraq's oil riches should be handled. Backed by Iran, SCIRI believes reserves should be nationalized and managed in the interests of the country's various communities. . . . The INC, for its part, believes that a private consortium should be set up to explore and extract oil. The consortium would include some of the world's biggest oil companies, such as ChevronTexaco, ExxonMobil and BP"—plus oil companies in France and Russia, provided they agreed in the U.N. Security Council to vote for war with Iraq.[31]

In December 2002, Robert Dreyfuss reported that the Bush administration actually preferred INC-supplied analyses of Iraq over the analysis coming from the CIA. "Even as it prepares for war against Iraq, the Pentagon is already engaged on a second front: its war against the Central Intelligence Agency," Dreyfuss wrote. "The Pentagon is bringing relentless pressure to bear on the agency to produce intelligence reports more supportive of war with Iraq. . . . Morale inside the U.S. national-security apparatus is said to be low, with career staffers feeling intimidated and pressured to justify the push for war." Much of the pro-war faction's information came from the INC, even though "most Iraq hands with long experience in dealing with that country's tumultuous politics consider the INC's intelligence-gathering abilities to be nearly nil. . . . The Pentagon's critics are appalled that intelligence provided by the INC might shape U.S. decisions about going to war against Baghdad. At the CIA and at the State Department, Ahmed Chalabi, the INC's leader, is viewed as the ineffectual head of a self-inflated and corrupt organization skilled at lobbying and public relations, but not much else."[32]

"The [INC's] intelligence isn't reliable at all," said Vincent Cannistraro, a former senior CIA official and counterterrorism expert. "Much of it is propaganda. Much of it is telling the Defense Department what they want to hear. And much of it is used to support Chalabi's own presidential ambitions. They make no distinction between intelligence and propaganda, using alleged informants and defectors who say what Chalabi wants them to say, [creating] cooked information that goes right into presidential and vice-presidential speeches."[33]

The Committee for the Invasion of Iraq

Preparatio[n]
for
prep
ira[q]

In November 2002, immediately following the mid-term elections, White House officials began working with a new group, the Committee for the Liberation of Iraq (CLI). CLI was actually a PNAC spin-off, sharing many of the same members and working closely with the American Enterprise Institute, the conservative think tank from which PNAC rented its office space.[34]

CLI's mission statement said that the group "was formed to promote regional peace, political freedom and international security by replacing the Saddam Hussein regime with a democratic government that respects the rights of the Iraqi people and ceases to threaten the community of nations."[35] CLI representatives made it clear that they wanted Saddam Hussein's overthrow, regardless of what weapons inspectors found or didn't find inside Iraq. "The problem in Iraq is not just Saddam Hussein's weapons—it is Saddam Hussein's regime," stated the CLI website.[36] The group used humanitarian language on its website and strove for a bipartisan appearance, with a few high-profile Democrats listed as members, including Joseph

Lieberman and Bob Kerrey. Overall, however, its leadership and affiliations were decidedly conservative, militaristic and very much in step with the Bush administration. CLI president Randy Scheunemann was a well-connected Republican military and foreign policy adviser who worked previously as national security adviser for Senators Trent Lott and Bob Dole. He also owned Orion Strategies, a small government-relations PR firm.[37]

CLI called itself "an independent entity," but it planned to "work closely with the administration," the *Washington Post's* Peter Slevin reported. "At a time when polls suggest declining enthusiasm for a U.S.-led military assault on Hussein, top officials will be urging opinion makers to focus on Hussein's actions in response to the United Nations resolution on weapons inspections—and on his past and present failings. They aim to regain momentum and prepare the political ground for his forcible ouster, if necessary."[38] According to former U.S. secretary of state George Schultz, who chaired CLI's advisory board, the committee "gets a lot of impetus from the White House." On November 15, CLI staffers met in the White House with National Security Adviser Condoleezza Rice. The *New York Times* reported that the "hawkish" group, "formed with the White House's tacit approval," was looking for additional funding for activities that would include "making contacts with journalists, holding dinner sessions with administration officials and meeting with editorial boards" across the country.[39]

"It is also encouraging its members to hold lectures around

the US, creating opportunities to penetrate local media markets," reported *PR Week*. "Members have already been interviewed on MSNBC and Fox News Channel, and articles have appeared in the *Washington Post* and the *New York Times*."[40]

And CLI was not the only group aggressively pushing for war on the talking-heads circuit. *PR Week* also reported that the Iraq Public Diplomacy Group, an initiative of the U.S. State Department, was providing media training to Iraqi dissidents to "help make the Bush administration's argument for the removal of Saddam Hussein."[41] The anti-Saddam Iraqis received coaching to help them look good on talk shows, give speeches and write newspaper opinion pieces. "We're going to put them on the front line of winning public hearts and minds," said a State Department official quoted by the *Los Angeles Times*. "It's one thing for an American to get up and talk about regime change in Iraq; it's quite another thing when Iraqis do it."[42] In addition to giving advice on *how* to speak effectively, the State Department also gave direction in *what* to say. "The message is democracy. The message is open and free elections. The message is what we have in our basic Bill of Rights," reported a State Department spokewoman quoted in *PR Week*.[43]

Muhammed Eshaiker, who serves on the board of the Iraqi Forum for Democracy, was one of the State Department trainees. "Iraqis in exile were not really taking advantage of the media opportunities," he explained. "We probably stumble and wait and say well, I mean what's the use—everybody knows [Hussein's] a criminal, so what's the use if we just add another story or another crime? But everything counts! . . . If we keep hammering on the same nail, the nail is going to find its way through."[44]

"Iraqis will welcome United States forces liberating them," the INC's Chalabi promised in an NBC interview on March 21, 2003, shortly after the war began. "I don't know if there are enough followers to do that now, but I think they will be happy to see the U.S. coming to help them liberate themselves and getting rid of Saddam."[45]

Trust Us, We're Experts

In addition to the Committee for the Liberation of Iraq, the Project for the New American Century and the American Enterprise Institute, several other organizations participated in the pro-war campaign. They included the Center for Strategic and International Studies (CSIS), the Washington Institute for Near East Policy, Middle East Forum, the Hudson Institute and the Hoover Institute, each of which shared a number of overlapping memberships and interests with the others. One thing that many had in common was their joint use of Benador Associates. Run by Eleana Benador, a Peruvian-born linguist by training, Benador Associates was a high-powered media relations company that acted as a sort of booking agent for experts on the Middle East and terrorism. Benador got her clients maximum exposure on talking-head television programs and with other speaking appearances, and placed their op-ed pieces in leading newspapers. She listed dozens of speakers on her website, many of whom played a prominent role in shaping the public debate over U.S. Middle East policy. Clients have included:

* Max Boot, an editorial features editor at the *Wall Street Journal* and author of *The Savage Wars of Peace: Small Wars and the Rise of American Power.* According to *Publisher's Weekly*, which reviewed the book, he "has a reputation as a fire-breathing polemicist and unabashed imperialist."
* Arnaud de Borchgrave, an editor at the conservative daily *Washington Times*, a newspaper owned by the Reverend Sun Myung Moon's Unification Church.[46] De Borchgrave also directs the Global Organized Crime Project at CSIS.
* Alexander M. Haig, Jr., former U.S. secretary of state under Ronald Reagan and a member of the Washington Institute for Near East Policy.
* Charles Krauthammer, a conservative columnist who contributes to publications including the *Washington Post* and the *Weekly Standard*.
* Michael A. Ledeen, another AEI fellow and a prominent figure in the Reagan administration's Iran-Contra scandal, who helped broker the covert arms deal between the U.S. and Iran.[47]
* Judith Miller, a reporter with the *New York Times*.
* Laurie Mylroie, author of *Study of Revenge: Saddam Hussein's Unfinished War Against America*, which was published

a year before the 9/11 attack and claimed that Saddam
Hussein was behind the 1993 bombing of the World Trade
Center. During the first U.S.-led war in the Persian Gulf,
Mylroie and Miller co-wrote a book titled *Saddam Hussein
and the Crisis in the Gulf.*

● Richard N. Perle, a longtime Washington cold warrior, adviser to the Bush administration, AEI fellow and member
of PNAC.

Like all of Benador's other clients, Laurie Mylroie vocally
supported war with Iraq in 2003—a striking contrast from the
position that she had taken in 1987, when she teamed up with
Daniel Pipes to co-author an essay for the *New Republic* titled
"Back Iraq: It's Time for a U.S. Tilt." Supporting Iraq was the
right policy, Mylroie and Pipes argued at the time, because the
"fall of the existing regime in Iraq would enormously enhance
Iranian influence, endanger the supply of oil, threaten pro-
American regimes throughout the area, and upset the Arab-
Israeli balance. . . . Helping Iraq militarily may offer the best
way for Washington to regain its position in Tehran. . . . Iraq is
now the de facto protector of the regional status quo. . . . If our
tilt toward Iraq is reciprocated, moreover, it could lay the basis
for a fruitful relationship in the longer term."[48]

During the buildup to war in 2003, Benador's clients received an extraordinary amount of media attention. In addition
to appearing on forums such as ABC, MSNBC, CNN and Fox
News, they published books and articles, testified before con-

gressional committees, and popped up frequently as guests at lunchtime gatherings in Washington. "I think it's safe to say we've used everyone on her list," said Tunku Varadarajan, the op-ed editor of the *Wall Street Journal,* adding that Benador called him nearly every day.[49]

As British journalist Brian Whitaker noted in August 2002, the attention that they received was all the more striking in comparison with the slight attention that media and policy makers paid to the 1,400 full-time faculty members who specialize in Middle East studies at American universities. "Those who work for US think tanks are often given university-style titles such as 'senior fellow,' or 'adjunct scholar,' but their research is very different from that of universities—it is entirely directed towards shaping government policy," Whitaker observed. "What nobody outside the think tanks knows, however, is who pays for this policy-shaping research."[50]

In addition to serving as a booking agent, Benador helped her clients package their message. In 2002 and 2003, for example, she advised them to downplay their enthusiasm for invading nations *other* than Iraq. Benador and several of her clients—including Ledeen, Perle and Pipes—also belong to the United States Committee for a Free Lebanon, which advocates the use of "overwhelming, non-surgical, nonproportional military force" against governments including Iran, Libya, Syria and Sudan.[51] Shortly after the war in Iraq commenced in March 2003, Joe Hagan of the *New York Observer* interviewed Benador about her work and noted that "her job was not only to work the phones for her clients, but sometimes to help polish their message":

> "There are some things, you have to just state them in a different way, in a slightly different way," she said. She described meeting with a new organization that plans to explore which rogue regime will be next in line for U.S. intervention following Iraq.
>
> "They said their agenda is to see who is next after Iraq," she said. "And I said, 'I don't think that's the right position, because "*Who* is next?" is like you're asking for more war.' And I said, 'So you can ask, "*What* is next? *What* is going to happen next?"' So I made them change that slightly.
>
> "See, it's a little word," she said, "but it makes a difference. If not, people get scared. And that's not the point. I'm just there looking after small details. Trying to avoid trouble for people and trying to make communication a little bit easier."[52]

Return of the Repressed

Meanwhile, two days before Saddam Hussein's regime crumbled in Baghdad, the *New York Times* reported that the Iraqi National Congress—the organization that the Rendon Group had carefully named and packaged 11 years earlier—had returned to the country. "Hundreds of Iraqi fighters opposed to

Saddam Hussein have been airlifted into southern Iraq to battle the remnants of his military and, more importantly, to serve
as the vanguard of a new national army," the article stated.[53]

"These are Iraqi citizens who want to fight for a free Iraq,
who will become basically the core of the new Iraqi army once
Iraq is free," said General Peter Pace, vice chairman of the Joint
Chiefs of Staff.[54]

The "Free Iraqi Forces," dressed in American military desert
fatigues and flown into a makeshift U.S. air base near Nasiriyah, were not your typical liberation fighters. For one thing,
there were no reports that they actually did any *fighting*, or that
they were even capable of it. Knight Ridder correspondent Sudarsan Raghavan described them as follows:

They are as young as 18 and as old as 55. About half come
from the United States, Britain, Iran, Norway, Canada, Jordan and a handful of other nations. A few came with their
children.

Some have missing teeth and grizzled beards. Others
have pot-shaped bellies and puff cigarettes as drill sergeants
bark orders.

"They are not the Wehrmacht," said Zaab Sethna, a senior adviser to Iraqi National Congress leader Ahmed Chalabi, referring to the German military of World War II. "But
their motivation is high, their energy is high."

The [Free Iraqi Forces] are the military wing of the Iraqi
National Congress, one of six groups vying to lead a new

Iraq. Chalabi, a London banker, stays in a damp warehouse on the base, along with his Harvard-educated daughter, Tamara, and aides.

After a recent patrol in a neighboring village, joyful fighters surrounded Chalabi and sang: "There is blood in our souls. We will redeem you, Dr. Chalabi."[55]

Chalabi, whose return marked his first opportunity to set foot in Baghdad since his exile in 1958, set up headquarters in the Hunting Club, a private enclave that was previously the club of Saddam Hussein's son Uday. "I am not a candidate for any position in the interim government," he said. "My role is to rebuild Iraq."[56] Simultaneously, however, his office began to take on the trappings of a government-in-waiting, as throngs of petitioners came clamoring for jobs and favors. "They believe Chalabi, who returned home last week after many years in exile, is America's man in Baghdad," reported the *Washington Post*. "Chalabi seems more than willing to play this role. He has been spending his time in meetings with delegations of tribal leaders, businessmen and even members of the deposed regime of Saddam Hussein trying to solve their problems. It's not clear on whose authority Chalabi is acting, but then, nothing is clear in the turmoil of postwar Iraq. He does have a liaison officer with him from the U.S. Army's Centcom, which suggests he has not lost his Pentagon patrons."[57]

As the war faded, Chalabi's name began popping up in more and more places. Top officials of the Saddam Hussein regime were reported to be surrendering to INC members attached to U.S. civil affairs units. In the city of Mosul, the *New York Times* reported, "Iraqi political parties have slowly begun opening up new offices this week. But only one group [Chalabi's] shares a base with American Special Forces soldiers, has a private army trained by the Americans and is guarding a local hospital alongside American troops."[58]

In May, longtime Chalabi aide Francis Brooke—a former Rendon employee—said that Chalabi might bow to popular pressure and agree to become Iraq's president after all. "George Washington turned it down many times," Brooke said, apparently without irony. "I wouldn't be surprised if the Iraqi people prevail on him."[59] On May 5, U.S. general Jay Garner named Chalabi as one of five Iraqis likely to be appointed as the nucleus of a new interim government.[60]

3. True Lies

AT A PRESS BRIEFING two weeks following the terrorist attacks of September 11, Defense Secretary Donald Rumsfeld had an exchange with a reporter that deserves to be quoted in some detail. In the context of the "war on terrorism," a reporter asked, "Will there be any circumstances, as you prosecute this campaign, in which anyone in the Department of Defense will be authorized to lie to the news media in order to increase the chances of success of a military operation or gain some other advantage over your adversaries?"

Rumsfeld replied:

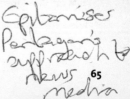
Epitomises
Pentagon's
approach to
news
media

Of course, this conjures up Winston Churchill's famous phrase when he said—don't quote me on this, OK. I don't want to be quoted on this, so don't quote me—he said, sometimes the truth is so precious it must be accompanied by a bodyguard of lies, talking about the invasion date and the invasion location, and indeed, they engaged not just in not talking about the date of the Normandy invasion or the location, whether it was to be Normandy Beach or just north off of Belgium, they actually engaged in a plan to confuse the Germans as to where it would happen. And they had a fake army under General Patton, and one thing and another.

That is a piece of history. And I bring it up just for the sake of background.

The answer to your question is no. I cannot imagine a situation. I don't recall that I've ever lied to the press. I don't intend to. And it seems to me that there will not be reason for it. There are dozens of ways to avoid having to put yourself in a position where you're lying. And I don't do it. And [Victoria Clarke] won't do it. And Admiral Quigley won't do it.

Reporter: That goes for everybody in the Department of Defense?

Rumsfeld: You've got to be kidding. (Laughter.)[1]

A few months later, the *New York Times* reported that a new group within the Pentagon, the Office of Strategic Influence (OSI), was "developing plans to provide news items, possibly even false ones, to foreign media organizations." Headed by Brigadier General Simon P. Worden, the OSI had a multimillion-dollar budget and "has begun circulating classified proposals calling for aggressive campaigns that use not only the foreign media and the Internet, but also covert operations," the *Times* stated. "General Worden envisions a broad mission ranging from 'black' campaigns that use disinformation and other covert activities to 'white' public affairs that rely on truthful news releases, Pentagon officials said. 'It goes from the blackest of black programs to the whitest of white,' a senior Pentagon official said."[2]

The proposal was controversial even within the military, where critics worried that it would undermine the Pentagon's credibility and blur the boundaries between covert operations and public relations. Moreover, disinformation planted in foreign media organizations could end up being published and broadcast to U.S. audiences. The *Times* report sparked an uproar in Congress and led to outraged newspaper editorials. Within a week, the White House closed down the OSI, disavowing any intent to ever use disinformation. Defense Secretary Donald Rumsfeld claimed that he had "never even seen the charter for the office," even though the OSI's assistant for operations said otherwise.[3]

In fact, Rumsfeld seemed to care quite a bit about preserving the functions of an office whose charter he claimed never to have seen. Nine months later, he made the following remark during an airplane flight to Chile: "And then there was the Office of Strategic Influence. You may recall that. And 'Oh, my goodness gracious, isn't that terrible, Henny Penny, the sky is going to fall.' I went down that next day and said fine, if you want to savage this thing, fine, I'll give you the corpse. There's the name. You can have the name, but I'm going to keep doing every single thing that needs to be done, and I have."[4]

The Mother of All Lies

The blurring of boundaries between truth and myth certainly did not begin with the current Bush administration. Disinformation has been a part of war since at least the days of Alexander the Great, who planted large breastplates of armor in the wake of his retreating troops to convince the enemy that his soldiers were giants. The story of Alexander's little trick is usually taught in the first day of class for soldiers who receive training in psychological operations (often contracted as "psyops").

A 1998 U.S. Air Force document titled *Information Operations* states, "Information operations apply across the range of military operations, from peace to all-out conflict. . . . It is important to stress that *information warfare* is a construct that operates across the spectrum, from peace to war, to allow the effective execution of Air Force responsibilities. . . . The execution of information operations in air, space, and cyberspace cross the spectrum of conflict." (Note the doublespeak involved in classifying "peace" as a "military operation.")

Information Operations includes sections titled "psychological operations," "electronic warfare," "information attack," "counterdeception" and "military deception." In today's world, it states, "There is a growing information infrastructure that transcends industry, the media, and the military and includes both government and nongovernment entities. It is characterized by a merging of civilian and military information networks and technologies. . . . In reality, a news broadcast, a diplomatic communiqué, and a military message ordering the execution of an operation *all* depend on the [global information infrastructure]." In this environment, psyops "are designed to convey selected information and indicators to foreign leaders and audiences to influence their emotions, motives, objective reasoning, and ultimately their behavior," while "military deception misleads adversaries, causing them to act in accordance with the originator's objectives." Indeed, it says, quoting Chinese military strategist Sun Tzu, "All warfare is based on deception."[5]

Inbro?

Babies from Incubators

A story of "babies torn from incubators" by Iraqi soldiers helped build public support for the first U.S. war in the Persian Gulf. The story was widely believed at the time of its telling and was not discredited until after the war ended. Since then, journalists and human rights organizations have investigated and concluded that the story was false. The episode has become infamous within the PR community itself, yet many members of the general public still believe that the story is true.

Following the August 2, 1990, invasion of Kuwait by Iraq, the United States needed to do a quick about-face. By then, Hussein had been a U.S. ally for nearly a decade, notwithstanding condemnations from international human rights groups.

Hill & Knowlton, then the world's largest PR firm, served as mastermind for a massive PR campaign to persuade Americans that they should support a war to reclaim the country from Iraq.[6] Much of the money for the pro-war marketing campaign came from the government-in-exile of Kuwait itself, which signed a contract with H&K nine days after Saddam's army marched into Kuwait. Hill & Knowlton created Citizens for a Free Kuwait, a classic PR front group designed to hide the campaign's sponsorship by the Kuwaiti government and its collusion with the Bush administration. Over the next six months, the Kuwaiti government channeled $11.9 million to Citizens for a Free Kuwait, whose only other funding totalled $17,861 from 78 individuals. Virtually all of the group's budget—$10.8 million—went to Hill & Knowlton in the form of fees.[7]

Documents filed with the U.S. Department of Justice showed that 119 H&K executives in 12 offices across the U.S. were overseeing the Kuwait account. The PR firm arranged media interviews for visiting Kuwaitis, organized a "National Free Kuwait Day" and other public rallies, distributed news releases and information kits, and assisted in the distribution to influential journalists and U.S. troops of more than 200,000 copies of a quickie 154-page book about Iraqi atrocities titled *The Rape of Kuwait*.[8] The scale of the Hill & Knowlton campaign awed even *O'Dwyer's PR Services Report*, one of the public relations industry's leading trade publications. Publisher Jack O'Dwyer wrote that Hill & Knowlton "has assumed a role in world affairs unprecedented for a PR firm. H&K has employed a stunning variety of opinion-forming devices and techniques to help keep US opinion on the side of the Kuwaitis. . . . The techniques range from full-scale press conferences showing torture and other abuses by the Iraqis to the distribution of tens of thousands of 'Free Kuwait' T-shirts and bumper stickers at college campuses across the US."[9]

Every big media event needs what journalists and flacks alike refer to as "the hook." An ideal hook becomes the central element of a story that makes it newsworthy, evokes a strong emotional response and sticks in the memory. For the Kuwaiti campaign, the hook came on October 10, 1990, when the Congressional Human Rights Caucus held a hearing on Capitol Hill that provided the first opportunity for formal presentations of Iraqi human rights violations. Outwardly, the hearing resembled an official congressional proceeding, but appearances were deceiving. Although the Human Rights Caucus was chaired by Congressmen Tom Lantos and John Porter, it was not an official congressional committee. Only a few observers noticed the significance of this detail. One of them was John MacArthur, author of *The Second Front*, which remains the best book written about the manipulation of the news media during the first Gulf War. "The Human Rights Caucus is not a committee of Congress, and therefore it is unencumbered by the legal accouterments that would make a witness hesitate before he or she lied," MacArthur observed. "Lying under oath in front of a congressional committee is a crime; lying from under the cover of anonymity to a caucus is merely public relations."[10]

The most emotionally moving testimony on October 10 came from a 15-year-old Kuwaiti girl, identified only by her first name, Nayirah. According to the Caucus, Nayirah's full name, as kept confidential to prevent Iraqi reprisals against her family in occupied Kuwait. Sobbing, she described what she had seen with her own eyes in a hospital in Kuwait City. Her written testimony was passed out in a media kit prepared by Citizens for a Free Kuwait. "I volunteered at the al-Addan hospital," Nayirah said. "While I was there, I saw the Iraqi soldiers come into the hospital with guns, and go into the room where . . . babies were in incubators. They took the babies out of the incubators, took the incubators, and left the babies on the cold floor to die." She went on to claim that this had happened to "hundreds" of babies.[11]

Three months passed between Nayirah's testimony and the start of the war. During those months, the story of babies torn from their incubators was repeated over and over. President Bush told the story. It was recited as fact in congressional testimony, on TV and radio talk shows, and at the U.N. Security Council. Amnesty International repeated the claim in a December 1990 human rights report, stating that "over 300 premature babies were reported to have died after Iraqi soldiers removed them from incubators, which were then looted."[12]

"Of all the accusations made against the dictator," MacArthur observed, "none had more impact on American public opinion than the one about Iraqi soldiers removing 312 babies from their incubators and leaving them to die on the cold hospital floors of Kuwait City."[13]

At the Human Rights Caucus, however, Hill & Knowlton and Congressman Lantos had failed to reveal that Nayirah was a member of the Kuwaiti Royal Family. Her father, in fact, was Saud Nasir al-Sabah, Kuwait's ambassador to the U.S., who sat listening in the hearing room during her testimony. The Caucus also failed to reveal that Hill & Knowlton vice president Lauri Fitz-Pegado had coached Nayirah's testimony.[14]

Following the war, human rights investigators attempted to confirm Nayirah's story and could find no witnesses or other evidence to support it. John Martin of *ABC World News Tonight* visited the al-Addan hospital and interviewed Dr. Mohammed Matar, director of Kuwait's primary health care system, and his wife, Dr. Fayeza Youssef, who ran the obstetrics unit at the maternity hospital. Nayirah's charges, they said, were false. In reality, there were only a handful of incubators in all of Kuwait, certainly not the "hundreds" that Nayirah had claimed, and no one had seen Iraqi troops yanking babies from incubators. "I think it was just something for propaganda," Matar said.[15]

Martin's reporting prompted a separate investigation by

Amnesty International, which had accepted the "babies torn from incubators" story at the time Nayirah gave her testimony. Amnesty International's investigators found "no reliable evidence" for the story and retracted their earlier report.[16] "We became convinced . . . that the story about babies dying in this way did not happen on the scale that was initially reported, if, indeed, it happened at all," said an Amnesty International spokesman.[17]

Middle East Watch, another human rights organization, also investigated the story and concluded that it was a hoax. Middle East Watch associate director Aziz Abu-Hamad, who led a three-week investigation in Kuwait following the war, stated, "Middle East Watch's own extensive research found no evidence to support the charge. After the liberation of Kuwait, we visited all Kuwaiti hospitals where such incidents were reported to have taken place. We interviewed doctors, nurses and administrators and checked hospital records. We also visited cemeteries and examined their registries. While we did find ample evidence of Iraqi atrocities in Kuwait, we found no evidence to support the charge that Iraqi soldiers pulled babies out of incubators and left them to die. Kuwaiti government witnesses who during the Iraqi occupation asserted the veracity of the incubator story have either changed their stories or were discredited. The propagation of false accounts of atrocities does a deep disservice to the cause of human rights. It diverts attention from the real violations that were committed by Iraqi forces in Kuwait, including the killing of hundreds and the detention of thousands of Kuwait citizens and others, hundreds of whom are still missing."[18]

Serving a Higher Truth

Why invent atrocity stories when Saddam Hussein's regime offered so many examples of *true* stories? There is no shortage of evidence that he was a brutal dictator responsible for the torture and death of thousands—in fact, hundreds of thousands—of innocent people.

One explanation might be that stories about "baby killers" are a staple of war propaganda. During the First World War, for example, the French and British spread stories (never documented or corroborated) claiming that German soldiers had bayoneted a two-year-old child and "chopped off the arms of a baby that clung to its mother's skirts"—a story that was embellished further when a French newspaper published a drawing depicting German soldiers eating the hands.[19]

If U.S. war planners wanted to hang the label of "baby killer" around Saddam's neck, though, they could have done it honestly. Women and children accounted for 75 percent of the estimated 5,000 people killed when he gassed his own citizens—Iraqi Kurds in the village of Halabja in 1988. The problem was that the Halabja incident and other uses of chemical weapons occurred *while Iraq was receiving military and economic support from the United States.* "By any measure, the American record on Halabja is shameful," said Joost R. Hiltermann of Human Rights Watch, which extensively investigated the Halabja incident. In fact, the U.S. State Department even "instructed its diplomats to say that Iran was partly to blame. The result of this stunning act of sophistry was that the international community failed to muster the will to condemn Iraq strongly for an act as heinous as the terrorist strike on the World Trade Center."[20]

During the buildup to war in 1990, the Halabja atrocity and the State Department's acquiescence were so recent that it would have been difficult for the first Bush administration to persuade anyone that its moral outrage was sincere. Telling the truth would have raised too many awkward questions. The pro-war camp wanted to tell the truth about the nature of Saddam Hussein's regime, but to protect itself from the full consequences of that truth, it needed what Churchill or Rumsfeld would call a "bodyguard of lies."

During the buildup to Operation Desert Storm, therefore, the first Bush administration avoided mentioning the Halabja incident, and reporters seldom mentioned it either. A search of the LexisNexis news database shows that Halabja was mentioned in 188 news stories in the United States in 1988 (the year that the incident occurred). It was rarely mentioned, however, in subsequent years—20 stories in 1989, and only 29 in 1990, the year that Saddam invaded Kuwait. Between the invasion of Kuwait on August 2, 1990, and the end of Operation

Desert Storm on February 27, 1991, Halabja received only 39 mentions. During the following decade, it barely averaged 16 mentions per year. During the presidential election year 2000, it got only 10 mentions. The story didn't really begin to circulate again in the U.S. media until September 2002, when the George W. Bush administration began its public push for war with Iraq. After that, mentions began to increase sharply. The Halabja incident was mentioned 57 times in the month of February 2003 alone. In March, the month that the war began, it was mentioned 145 times. By then, nearly 15 years had passed, memories had faded, and it was safe to talk about Saddam's gassing of Iraqi citizens. Only a few of the journalists who wrote about Halabja in 2002 and 2003 bothered to mention that Saddam committed his worst atrocities while the president's father was showering him with financial aid.

The pattern was quite different with regard to Nayirah's story of "babies pulled from incubators." According to the same Lexis-Nexis database, the babies-from-incubators story received 138 mentions during the seven months between the invasion of Kuwait and the end of Operation Desert Storm. Shortly after the war ended, journalists began debunking the original version when they visited Kuwaiti hospitals and were told by hospital personnel that the story was a fabrication. After 1992, the story disappeared almost entirely, averaging fewer than ten mentions per year for the next decade. However, the babies-from-incubators story did resurface briefly in December 2002, when HBO television premiered a "based on a true story" docudrama titled

"Live From Baghdad," which recounted the adventures of Peter Arnett and other CNN reporters during Operation Desert Storm. "Live From Baghdad" included actual footage of Nayirah delivering her false testimony and left viewers with the impression that the story was true. In response to complaints generated by the media-watch organization FAIR, HBO added a disclaimer at the end of the credits, which admits that "allegations of Iraqi soldiers taking babies from incubators . . . were never substantiated."[21] Of course, that disclaimer was noticed only by those few viewers who read all the credits. Prior to the addition of the disclaimer, *Washington Post* TV critic Tom Shales reviewed "Live From Baghdad" and wrote, "The horror wreaked on Kuwait is brought back vividly during a sequence in which [CNN producer Robert] Wiener and his team travel to Kuwait to investigate allegations that Iraqi troops had ripped babies out of incubators as part of their plundering—remember?"[22]

It may be unfair to single out Shales for his part in "remembering" an incident that never happened. Nayirah's tale of the incubators is simply one more illustration of the principle, long understood by propagandists, that a lie which is repeated often enough becomes widely accepted as truth.

Bullet Points

In an October 2002 opinion poll by the Pew Research Center for the People and the Press, 66 percent of Americans said that they believed Saddam Hussein was involved in the September 11 attacks on the United States, while 79 percent believed that Iraq already possessed, or was close to possessing, nuclear weapons. The same poll looked at *why* many people supported war and found that the main reason was their belief that it would reduce the threat of terrorism. The principal reason cited by 25 percent of war supporters related to their perceptions of Hussein or the nature of his regime (he's "evil," a "madman," "represses his own people"). However, more than twice that number—60 percent—gave a reason related to their concerns stemming from 9/11 (getting rid of weapons of mass destruction, preventing future terrorism).[23]

In January 2003, Knight Ridder Newspapers conducted its own, separate opinion poll. "Two-thirds of the respondents said they thought they had a good grasp of the issues surrounding the Iraqi crisis, but closer questioning revealed large gaps in that knowledge," it reported. "For instance, half of those surveyed said one or more of the Sept. 11 terrorist hijackers were Iraqi citizens. In fact, none was." Moreover, "The informed public is considerably less hawkish about war with Iraq than the public as a whole. Those who show themselves to be most knowledgeable about the Iraq situation are significantly less likely to support military action, either to remove Saddam from power or to disarm Iraq."[24]

This gap between reality and public opinion was not an accident. If the public had possessed a more accurate understanding of the facts, more people would probably have seen a "pre-emptive" war with Iraq as unwise and unwarranted. The public's erroneous beliefs developed much the same way that the babies-from-incubators story came to be accepted as truth: through a steady drumbeat of allegations and insinuations from the Bush administration, pro-war think tanks and commentators—statements that were, as we shall see, often false or misleading and whose purpose was to create the impression that Iraq posed an imminent peril.

Baghdad's Bombs

Of all the Bush administration's arguments in support of war with Iraq, the strongest was its claim that Iraq possessed or might acquire weapons of mass destruction. Iraq did indeed possess chemical and biological weapons at the time of Operation Desert Storm (many of them supplied by the United States and other Western nations), and it had used chemical weapons in genocidal attacks on its own people as well as the people of Iran.[25] Saddam Hussein also had attempted to develop nuclear weapons.[26] International pressure following Desert Storm forced the destruction of many weapons in the Iraqi arsenal, but the regime failed to document their complete destruction, so it was certainly possible that some remained.[27]

One of the striking ironies of the debate over Iraq is that Saddam Hussein's own propaganda may have helped reinforce perceptions that it posed an imminent threat. As twentieth-century

French playwright Jean Anouilh once observed, "Propaganda is a soft weapon; hold it in your hands too long, and it will move about like a snake, and strike the other way." Following Iraq's defeat at the end of Desert Storm, many of its banned weapons were dismantled, says *Washington Post* reporter Barton Gellman, who has reported extensively on the activities of the United Nations Special Commission (UNSCOM) and its investigations into Iraqi weapons. However, this happened not because Saddam's character suddenly improved but because he wanted to create the *appearance* of compliance so that he could preserve the wherewithal to produce similar weapons in the future. "They had used chemical weapons extensively in the Iran-Iraq War, so they couldn't say they didn't have that program," Gellman said. "They decided to sacrifice their oldest and least sophisticated chemical weapons. They were available in quantity to do so. They made a great show of bringing these to UNSCOM. UNSCOM laid dynamite across them and blew them up and buried them in pits and everyone felt they were making great progress. But they were also carefully culling their files to make sure that the advanced binary chemical weapons, that the entire existence of a biological program, that some of their missile facilities, and the existence of any nuclear weapons program at all, were carefully hidden."[28]

In 1995, however, Iraq's man in charge of its advanced weapons programs—Hussein Kamel, Saddam's son-in-law—defected to Jordan, carrying insider information that shocked weapons inspectors and led to much more stringent enforce-

ment actions. At that point, Gellman says, "Iraq had a big problem on its hands, because it needed a new explanation for all
this. And the explanation they hit upon was: 'We are shocked,
shocked, to discover that under our very noses, Kamel all this
time has been hiding all kinds of weapons and documentation.
We've discovered it on his chicken farm, and here it is. You may
have it all.' And they deliver to UNSCOM one million pages of
newly-declared documents, which show a lot of biological
weapons programs, which show a lot more chemical weapons
programs, which show material shortfalls, which show missile
stuff, which show nuclear stuff."[29]

During the buildup to war, Kamel's defection was cited re-
peatedly by President Bush and other administration officials as
evidence that Iraq had not disarmed and that inspections were
not working. "It took four years for Iraq to finally admit that it
had produced four tons of the deadly nerve agent, VX," said
Colin Powell in his February 5, 2003, presentation to the U.N.
Security Council. "The admission only came out after inspectors collected documentation as a result of the defection of
Hussein Kamel." Vice President Dick Cheney said that Kamel's
story "should serve as a reminder to all that we often learned
more as the result of defections than we learned from the inspection regime itself."

This was all true, as far as it went, but there was just one
problem. Kamel had *also* told interrogators that Iraq's actual
weapons were all destroyed shortly after the end of the first
Gulf War. On March 3, 2003, *Newsweek* magazine's John Barry

reported obtaining a transcript of Kamel's interrogation by UNSCOM investigator Nikita Smidovich and Maurizio Zifferero of the International Atomic Energy Agency (IAEA), in which Kamel told inspectors that "after the Gulf War, Iraq destroyed all its chemical and biological weapons stocks and the missiles to deliver them." All that remained, he said, were "hidden blueprints, computer disks, microfiches" and production molds. The weapons were destroyed secretly to hide their existence from inspectors, in the hopes of someday resuming production after inspections had finished. The CIA and British MI6 were told the same story, Barry reported, and "a military aide who defected with Kamel . . . backed Kamel's assertions about the destruction of WMD stocks."[30] The following excerpt from the transcript tells the story:

SMIDOVICH (with regard to biological weapons): Were weapons and agents destroyed?

KAMEL: Nothing remained.

SMIDOVICH: Was it before or after inspections started?

KAMEL: After visits of inspection teams. You have important role in Iraq with this. You should not underestimate yourself. You are very effective in Iraq. . . .

Smidovich asked about Iraq's VX chemical weapons program.

KAMEL: They put it in bombs during last days of the Iran-Iraq war. They were not used and the program was terminated.

During the Gulf War (Operation Desert Storm), there was no intention to use chemical weapons as the Allied force was overwhelming. . . . We gave instructions not to produce chemical weapons. I don't remember resumption of chemical weapon production before the Gulf War. Maybe it was only minimal production and filling. But there was no decision to use chemical weapons for fear of retaliation. They realized that if chemical weapons were used, retaliation would be nuclear. . . . All chemical weapons were destroyed. I ordered destruction of all chemical weapons. All weapons— biological, chemical, missile, nuclear—were destroyed.[31]

Of course, defectors from Iraq cannot be counted on to be 100 percent truthful, but nevertheless the gap is striking between what Kamel actually said and the way Bush administration officials described his revelations to the public. Moreover, Kamel's defection led to intensified efforts to find and destroy remaining components of Iraq's weapons program. Given the regime's prior history of concealing and destroying information, it is impossible to know with certainty whether the weapons were all destroyed by the time UNSCOM inspectors left Iraq in 1998. Individual inspectors have themselves reached differing conclusions. Scott Ritter, an UNSCOM inspector who resigned to protest what he regarded as inadequate enforcement, later came to believe that inspections had been successful in eliminating most of the weapons. His assessment, published in the *Boston Globe* in July 2002, was as follows:

While we were never able to provide 100 percent certainty regarding the disposition of Iraq's proscribed weaponry, we did ascertain a 90 to 95 percent level of verified disarmament. This figure takes into account the destruction or dismantling of every major factory associated with prohibited weapons manufacture, all significant items of production equipment, and the majority of the weapons and agent produced by Iraq.

With the exception of mustard agent, all chemical agent produced by Iraq prior to 1990 would have degraded within five years. . . . The same holds true for biological agent, which would have been neutralized through natural processes within three years of manufacture. Effective monitoring inspections, fully implemented from 1994–1998 without any significant obstruction from Iraq, never once detected any evidence of retained proscribed activity or effort by Iraq to reconstitute that capability which had been eliminated through inspections.

In direct contrast to these findings, the Bush administration provides only speculation, failing to detail any factually based information to bolster its claims concerning Iraq's continued possession of or ongoing efforts to acquire weapons of mass destruction. To date no one has held the Bush administration accountable for its unwillingness—or inability—to provide such evidence.[32]

It should be noted that Ritter's perspective was controversial and differed from the assessment of several other weapons inspectors. The test of whether Iraq possessed chemical and biological weapons worth fighting a war over will ultimately depend on what is actually found as U.S. troops comb through the country. With regard to nuclear weapons, however, the evidence is already fairly clear that the Bush administration has engaged in selective interpretation and distortions of the known record.

Here too, no one disputes that Saddam desired nuclear weapons and made active attempts to develop them prior to the first Gulf War. The war and its aftermath, however, led to the destruction of whatever facilities he did have along with subsequent weapons inspections making it difficult for him to restart the program. (It is considerably harder to conceal a nuclear weapons program than it is to conceal efforts to develop chemical and biological weapons.) Distortions from the Bush administration include the following:

* On September 7, 2002, Bush cited a report by the International Atomic Energy Agency that he said proved that the Iraqis were on the brink of developing nuclear weapons. "I would remind you that when the inspectors first went into Iraq and were denied, finally denied access, a report came out of the Atomic—the IAEA—that they were six months away from developing a weapon," he said. "I don't know what more evidence we need."[33] Actually, no such report existed. The IAEA did issue a report in 1998, around the time weapons inspectors were denied access to Iraq, but

what it said was, "Based on all credible information to date, the IAEA has found no indication of Iraq having achieved its program goal of producing nuclear weapons or of Iraq having retained a physical capability for the production of weapon-useable nuclear material or having clandestinely obtained such material." Responding to the Bush speech, IAEA chief spokesman Mark Gwozdecky said, "There's never been a report like that issued from this agency."[34]

- In his September 12, 2002, address to the United Nations, Bush spoke ominously of Iraq's "continued appetite" for nuclear bombs, pointing to the regime's purchase of thousands of high-strength aluminum tubes, which he said were "used to enrich uranium for nuclear weapons."[35] In fact, the IAEA said in a January 2003 assessment, the size of the tubes made them ill-suited for uranium enrichment, but they were identical to tubes that Iraq had used previously to make conventional artillery rockets.[36] Nevertheless, Colin Powell repeated the aluminum-tubes charge in his speech to the U.N. on February 5, 2003.

- In an October 7, 2002, speech to the nation, Bush warned that Iraq has a growing fleet of unmanned aircraft that could be fitted with chemical or biological weapons and used "for missions targeting the United States." Actually, the aircraft lacked the range to reach the United States.[37]

- In the same speech, Bush also stated that in 1998, "information from a high-ranking Iraqi nuclear engineer who had defected revealed that despite his public promises,

Saddam Hussein had ordered his nuclear program to continue."[38] Bush's statement implied that this information
was current as of 1998. In fact, the nuclear defector to
whom he referred was Khidhir Hamza, who had actually
retired from Iraq's nuclear program in 1991 and fled the
country in 1995.[39] Bush also neglected to note that Hussein Kamel, whose earlier defection and debriefing by
UNSCOM investigators is described previously, told investigators during the same interview that he regarded Hamza
as a "professional liar."[40]

- Finally, in Bush's Spring 2003 State of the Union speech,
he cited alleged documents showing that Iraq had attempted to buy 500 tons of uranium from the country of
Niger. However, officials of the International Atomic Energy Agency (IAEA) looked at the documents and concluded that they were crude fakes. A team of forensics
experts examined the documents and agreed unanimously.[41] Congressman Henry Waxman (D–California),
who voted in favor of Bush's war initiative, was disturbed by
these disclosures and expressed concern in a letter to the
White House in which he noted that the CIA had already
warned in 2001 that the documents were fakes. "These
facts raise troubling questions," Waxman wrote. "It appears
that at the same time you, Secretary Rumsfeld, and State
Department officials were citing Iraq's efforts to obtain uranium from Africa as a crucial part of the case against Iraq,
U.S. intelligence officials regarded this very same evidence

as unreliable. If true, this is deeply disturbing: it would mean that your Administration asked the U.N. Security Council, the Congress, and the American people to rely on information that your own experts knew was not credible."[42]

The idea that Iraq's weapons of mass destruction posed an imminent threat also contrasts strangely with the Bush administration's low-key response to the news that North Korea had indeed developed nuclear weapons and possessed the means to fire them at the United States. "North Korea already has 100 missiles that have a range of 1,000 kilometers," said U.S. senator Bob Graham (D–Florida) in an October 2002 television interview. "They're working on a missile that would have range sufficient to reach the West Coast of the United States. They have two nuclear weapons today, and . . . they could start adding nuclear weapons. Conversely, Saddam Hussein, we have no reason to believe that he has nuclear weapons, although he is striving to secure them. And he has relatively limited, in range and number, methods of delivery of those. So, if you put the two, North Korea and Iraq, on the scales and ask the question, which today is the greater threat to the people of the United States of America, I would answer the question: North Korea."[43]

Graham, who chaired the Senate Intelligence Committee, was so baffled by the contradictory assessments of Iraq coming from different agencies that in July 2002 he asked the CIA to come up with a report on the likelihood that Saddam Hussein would use weapons of mass destruction. When asked this question directly, a senior CIA intelligence witness responded that the likelihood was "low" for the "foreseeable future."[44] Like many of the analyses that conflicted with the drive for war, this statement from the CIA went largely unreported.

Dropping the Bombshell

The gap between rhetoric and reality about Iraq's weaponry became evident with the launch of war in March 2003. As U.S. forces blew past Iraq's military, U.S. and Kuwaiti officials spoke darkly about reports that Iraq had allegedly fired two banned Scud missiles at U.S. positions inside Kuwait. Neither missile produced any casualties, but hundreds of newspapers and other media reported ominously on the alleged Scud attack. "The very missiles Saddam Hussein fired at U.S. forces in Kuwait appear to have been the same weapons he either claimed not to possess or agreed to destroy," reported the Associated Press on March 21, 2003. "The first salvos were both a telling sign of Iraq's hidden weapons and a reminder that Saddam still has the capability of delivering chemical or biological warheads."[45] This round of warnings ended when Kuwaiti and U.S. officials had to withdraw their claim that Scuds had been used.[46] By war's end, Iraq had managed to fire only 20 missiles that landed outside its own borders. Most fell harmlessly into the Persian Gulf or the desert. Only one caused minor injuries, when it landed in front of a Kuwaiti shopping center.[47] The total number of banned weapons used by Iraq during the entire war appears to be zero.

As late as September 2002, a British report estimated that Iraq might possess up to 20 banned Scud missiles. If that estimate were true, it would have been less than one-fourth of the 88 Scuds that Iraq actually fired during Desert Storm. And even if Hussein still possessed Scuds, weapons specialist John Clearwater said, it was doubtful that they still functioned, noting that Iraqis have not been able to fire and test the missiles or obtain replacement parts for them for more than a decade. "These missiles have a short shelf life," said Clearwater, who has written three books on nuclear weapons and cruise missiles. "The longer you go without testing, the lower confidence you have in them."[48]

A hypothetical arsenal of 20 Scuds also pales in comparison with the number of real missiles that the United States launched directly into Baghdad on the *first day* of its "Shock and Awe" bombing campaign. British and U.S. forces began the war possessing 3,500 Tomahawk missiles. By the end of the war, they had fired 800 Tomahawks, more than 14,000 precision-guided munitions and an unspecified number of cluster bombs.[49]

Iraq and Al Qaeda

The idea of an alliance between Al Qaeda and Iraq was unlikely, since Osama bin Laden's hatred for the "infidel" regime of Saddam Hussein was long-standing and well known before September 11. Much of the public speculation about a link between Al Qaeda and Iraq was based on an alleged meeting between 9/11 hijacker Mohammed Atta and Iraqi intelligence officials that supposedly took place in Prague, the Czech Republic, between the dates of April 8 and 11, 2001.

Reports of this meeting first came from Czech officials in October 2001, during the period of intense speculation that followed the terrorist attacks. According to the Czech interior minister, Atta had met with Ahmed Khalil Ibrahim Samir al-Ani, a second consul at the Iraqi Embassy. According to Czech intelligence, however, the factual basis for the story was thin from the beginning. Its sole source was a single Arab émigré, who came forward with the information only after 9/11, when photographs of Atta appeared in the local Prague press. As the *New York Times* reported in December 2001, the story may have been simply a case of mistaken identity, since al-Ani "had a business selling cars and met frequently with a used car dealer from Germany who bore a striking resemblance to Mr. Atta."[50]

The story was thoroughly investigated by the FBI in the United States. "We ran down literally hundreds of thousands of leads and checked every record we could get our hands on," FBI director Robert Mueller said in an April 2002 speech in San Francisco. The records revealed that Atta was in Virginia Beach, Virginia, in early April, during the time he supposedly met al-Ani in Prague.[51]

After conducting his own separate investigations, Czech president Vaclav Havel laid the story to rest. The *Times* reported in 2002 that Havel "has quietly told the White House he has concluded that there is no evidence to confirm earlier reports that Mohammed Atta, the leader in the Sept. 11 attacks, met with an Iraqi intelligence official in Prague." Havel did this quietly "to avoid embarrassing" the other Czech officials who had previously given credibility to the story. "Today, other Czech officials say they have no evidence that Mr. Atta was even in the country in April 2001," the *Times* reported.[52]

Despite the lack of any credible evidence that the Atta-Iraq meeting ever occurred, Bush administration officials continued to promote the rumor, playing a delicate game of not-quite-lying insinuations. In February 2002, for example, *San Francisco Chronicle* reporter Robert Collier interviewed Deputy Defense Secretary Paul Wolfowitz, a leading advocate of war with Iraq. "Have you seen any convincing evidence to link Iraq to Al Qaeda or its international network?" Collier asked.

"A lot of this stuff is classified and I really can't get into discussing it," Wolfowitz said, adding, "We also know that there are things that haven't been explained . . . like the meeting of Mohammed Atta with Iraqi officials in Prague. It just comes back to the fact that—"

"Which now is alleged, right?" Collier said. "There is some doubt to that?"

"Now this gets you into classified areas again," Wolfowitz replied. "I think the point, which I do think is fundamental, is that, the premise of your question seems to be, we wait for proof beyond a reasonable doubt. I think the premise of a policy has to be, we can't afford to wait for proof beyond a reasonable doubt."[53]

Wolfowitz's performance typifies the administration's handling of the Atta-in-Prague story. Using vague references to "classified" information, he avoided specifics, while dismissing requests for actual *proof* as the bureaucratic concern of overly legalistic pencil-pushers. The pattern continued throughout a variety of subsequent pronouncements:

- In May 2002, William Safire, the conservative *New York Times* columnist and Iraq War hawk, cited an unnamed "senior Bush administration official" who told him, "You cannot say the Czech report about a meeting in 2001 between Atta and the Iraqi is discredited or disproven in any way. The Czechs stand by it and we're still in the process of pursuing it and sorting out the timing and venue."

- In July 2002, Donald Rumsfeld told a news conference that Iraq had "a relationship" with Al Qaeda but declined to be more specific.[54] The following month, the *Los Angeles Times* reported an interview with yet another unnamed "senior Bush administration official" who said that evidence of an Atta meeting in Prague "holds up," adding, "We're going to talk more about this case."[55]

- In September 2002, defense department adviser Richard Perle was quoted in an Italian business publication as saying that Atta met personally with Saddam Hussein himself. "Mohammed Atta met Saddam Hussein in Baghdad prior to September 11," Perle said. "We have proof of that, and we are sure he wasn't just there for a holiday."[56] (Since then, nothing whatsoever has been heard about the alleged "proof.")

- On September 8, 2002, Vice President Dick Cheney was interviewed on *Meet the Press*. "There has been reporting," he said, "that suggests that there have been a number of contacts over the years. We've seen in connection with the hijackers, of course, Mohammed Atta, who was the lead hijacker, did apparently travel to Prague on a number of occasions. And on at least one occasion, we have reporting that places him in Prague with a senior Iraqi intelligence official a few months before the attack on the World Trade Center."[57]

- "We know that Iraq and the Al Qaeda terrorist network share a common enemy," Bush himself said in an October 7, 2002, speech to the nation. In the same speech, he also mentioned "one very senior al Qaeda leader who received medical treatment in Baghdad this year." However, he did not mention that the terrorist in question, Abu Musab Zarqawi, was no longer in Iraq and that there was no hard evidence Hussein's government knew he was there or had contact with him. At an election campaign rally a week later, Bush said that Saddam was "a man who, in my judgment, would like to use Al Qaeda as a forward army."[58]

Like Nayirah's babies-from-incubators story, the Atta-in-Prague story acquired solidity in the minds of the public through sheer repetition. Each new whisper from a Bush team insider yielded a fresh harvest of newspaper editorials, I-told-you-so's and speculation on the Internet. Simply by mentioning Iraq and Al Qaeda together in the same sentence, over and over, the message got through. Where there is smoke, people were led to believe, there must be fire. But actually, there was only smoke.

Term Paper Time

The attempt to fabricate evidence of Iraq links to Al Qaeda lay at the heart of a scandal in England in February 2003, following the disclosure that much of the British government's published dossier on Iraq was actually plagiarized. Touted as an analysis by the British MI6 spy agency, the British dossier, titled "Iraq—Its Infrastructure of Concealment, Deception and Intimidation,"[59] was cited as evidence against Iraq by U.S. secretary of state Colin Powell in his February 5 address to the U.N. Security Council. "I would call my colleagues' attention to the fine paper that the United Kingdom distributed . . . which describes in exquisite detail Iraqi deception activities," Powell said.[60]

Upon reading the document, however, Cambridge University professor Glen Rangwala "found it quite startling when I realized that I'd read most of it before" in the *Middle East Review of International Affairs*, a publication that is also distributed on the Internet. Further investigation revealed that the bulk of the 19-page British dossier (pages 6 through 16) had actually been lifted from a paper titled "Iraq's Security and Intelligence Network: A Guide and Analysis,"[61] written by Dr. Ibrahim al-Marashi, a post-graduate student living in California.[62] The dossier had actually *not* been produced by MI6 but by junior aides to Alastair Campbell, the chief press secretary for British prime minister Tony Blair.[63] Confronted by al-Marashi's paper, embarrassed aides admitted that in their rush to cobble together a report, they had cut and pasted his material without permission or attribution, right down to his typographical errors.[64] Far from being an up-to-date analysis, al-Marashi's thesis was based mostly on Iraqi documents from 1991 or earlier—information that was more than a decade old. Further scrutiny found that other parts of the British dossier were lifted from *Jane's Intelligence Review*, part of the *Jane's* series of trade publications for soldiers and military contractors. One of the *Jane's* articles had been written by Ken Gause. Two others were by Sean Boyne, an analyst opposed to war with Iraq.[65]

The dossier was "obviously part of the Prime Minister's propaganda campaign," said Charles Heyman, editor of *Jane's World Armies*. "The intelligence services were not involved— I've had two people phoning me today to say, 'Look, we had nothing to do with it.'"[66]

"When the scandal broke in the UK media, the Blair administration appeared incompetent at best and, at worst, dishonest," observed *Jane's Intelligence Digest*. "In fact, much of the data contained in the report is reliable and accurate. Dr. Ibrahim al-Marashi, Sean Boyne and Ken Gause—authors whose previously published material in the *Middle East Review of International Affairs* and *Jane's Intelligence Review* was copied into the British Iraq dossier—are all well-respected analysts in their respective fields. More controversial, however, are passages that have been rewritten or interpolated into this material to strengthen the allegation being made by the USA and the UK that Iraq has been actively supporting international terrorism."[67]

There is a reason why Tony Blair's spin doctors avoided using their own spy agency to produce the report. Actually, MI6 analysts *disagreed* with Blair's public position, and they made this clear by leaking an official British intelligence report to BBC on the day that Colin Powell gave his speech to the United Nations. The leaked MI6 report explicitly contradicted the government's public position. It stated that there were no known links between Iraq and the Al Qaeda network, because Osama bin Laden's "aims are in ideological conflict with present day Iraq."[68]

During Powell's speech, he also described a compound in northeastern Iraq, run by the Islamic terrorist group Ansar al-Islam, as a "terrorist chemicals and poisons factory." When reporter Luke Harding of the *Observer*, a British daily, visited the site three days later, however, he reported finding "nothing of the kind." Describing the site as a "shabby military compound at the foot of a large snow-covered mountain," Harding said that it was "a dilapidated collection of concrete outbuildings at the foot of a grassy sloping hill. Behind the barbed wire, and a courtyard strewn with broken rocket parts, are a few empty concrete houses. There is a bakery. There is no sign of chemical weapons anywhere—only the smell of paraffin and vegetable ghee used for cooking." Harding added that the people of the town of Khurmal, located about five kilometers away from the compound, were fearful of an American military strike once the war began, "since Mr. Powell gave their town's name to the alleged chemical weapons site."[69] And in fact, Khurmal was bombed by U.S. cruise missiles on the first weekend after the war with Iraq began, killing 45 villagers.[70]

Patterns of Global Terrorism

The State Department's annual "Patterns of Global Terrorism" report, issued in May 2002, makes interesting reading in contrast to the Bush administration's claim that Iraq was the leading world terrorist threat.

According to "Patterns of Global Terrorism," Iraq's role as a state sponsor of terrorism consisted of being "the only Arab-Muslim country that did not condemn the September 11 attacks against the United States."[71] Also, Iraq provided safe haven to a number of Palestinian organizations involved with the *intifada*, such as the Popular Front for the Liberation of

Palestine (PFLP). Other terrorist groups that Iraq was reported to support included the Kurdish Workers Party (PKK) and the Mujahedin-e-Khalq (MEK). In both of these cases, the terrorist link requires some qualification. The PKK, a Marxist political party that supports Kurdish separatism in Turkey, publicly abandoned armed struggle in 1999.[72] The MEK is an armed guerrilla force that has been trying to overthrow the government of Iran. In all of these cases, Iraqi support for these groups reflects rivalries with its next-door neighbors and does not differ substantially from the type of support for terrorist groups that other governments practice in the region. According to "Patterns of Global Terrorism," in fact, it was *Iran*, not Iraq, that "remained the most active state sponsor of terrorism in 2001"—a title that Iran has held for several years running. But if that's the case, why such a rush to go to war with *Iraq*?

Even the State Department report was heavily influenced by spin. While condemning terrorism by Iran, Iraq and other longtime U.S. adversaries, "Patterns of Global Terrorism" praises allies such as Saudi Arabia, which it says have "played strong roles in the International Coalition against terrorism. In addition to condemning the September 11 attacks publicly, these governments took positive steps to halt the flow of terrorism financing and, in some cases, authorized basing and/or overflight provisions. In several cases, they did so despite popular disquiet over their governments' military support for Operation Enduring Freedom." Beneath a photograph of U.S. secretary of state Colin Powell shaking hands with Saudi Crown Prince Abdullah, the report acknowledges that laws against solicitation of funds for terrorists "were not scrupulously enforced in the past," but says that the Saudis have "agreed to cooperate with U.S. investigators."[73]

The irony in all this, of course, is that 15 of the 19 hijackers who flew the planes on September 11 were Saudi citizens, and links between the Saudi regime and Al Qaeda are much easier to draw than links between Iraq and Al Qaeda. Osama bin Laden and his terror network belong to a specific Muslim doctrinal school, Wahhabi fundamentalism, which is much more ideologically severe than the religion practiced by most Muslims throughout the world and which certainly differs from the largely secular ideology of Saddam Hussein's Ba'ath Party. However, Wahhabi provides the religious and ideological underpinnings of the absolute monarchy that rules Saudi Arabia with an iron fist. Human rights groups such as Amnesty International have pointed to the country's numerous cases of arbitrary arrest, prolonged detention and physical abuse of prisoners, which security forces commit with the acquiescence of the government.[74] In addition, the government prohibits or restricts freedom of speech, the press, assembly, association and religion. Partly as a release valve for domestic dissatisfaction with the oppressive nature of the Saudi regime, the monarchy tolerates and even encourages anti-Semitism and America-bashing that scapegoats Israel and the United States for all the problems of the region.[75]

"It is worth stating clearly and unambiguously what official

U.S. government spokespersons have not," stated "Terrorist Financing," an October 2002 report sponsored by the Council on Foreign Relations. "For years, individuals and charities based in Saudi Arabia have been the most important source of funds for Al Qaeda, and for years the Saudi officials have turned a blind eye to this problem. This is hardly surprising since Saudi Arabia possesses the greatest concentration of wealth in the region; Saudi nationals and charities were previously the most important sources of funds for the mujahideen [Islamic fundamentalists who fought the Soviet occupation of Afghanistan]; Saudi nationals have always constituted a disproportionate percentage of Al Qaeda's own membership; and Al Qaeda's political message has long focused on issues of particular interest to Saudi nationals, especially those who are disenchanted with their own government."[76]

In fact, it appears that some of those Saudi officials did more than merely turn a blind eye. In November 2002, the FBI investigated charitable payments by Haifa Al-Faisal, the wife of the Saudi ambassador to the United States, Prince Bandar bin Sultan. Beginning in early 2000, $3,500 a month flowed from Al-Faisal to two Saudi students in the United States who provided assistance to some of the 9/11 hijackers. One of the students who received the money threw a welcoming party for the hijackers upon their arrival in San Diego, paid their rent and guaranteed their lease on an apartment next door to his own. The other student, a known Al Qaeda sympathizer, also befriended the hijackers prior to their awful deed. At a party after the attacks, he "celebrated the heroes of September 11," openly talking about "what a wonderful, glorious day it had been."[77]

Princess Haifa did not send money directly to the hijackers, and there is no evidence that she had any prior knowledge of their plans. Nevertheless, the Bush administration's willingness to accept her explanations at face value contrasts strikingly with the enthusiasm with which the Bush administration pursued every slim thread that might connect Iraq to Al Qaeda. It handled the news about Haifa Al-Faisal's payments by urging people not to jump to conclusions. White House spokesman Ari Fleischer responded to the news by saying, "Saudi Arabia is a good partner in the war against terrorism but can do more."[78]

The Search for the Real Killers

Several investigators—including Joel Mowbray of the conservative *National Review*,[79] leftist BBC reporter Greg Palast,[80] and an investigative team at the *Boston Herald*[81]—have found evidence of links between prominent Saudis and the financing of Al Qaeda. Matthew Levitt, a senior fellow in terrorism studies at the Washington Institute for Near East Policy, says that much of Al Qaeda's funding has come through charities "closely linked to the Saudi government and royal family," including the Al-Haramain Islamic Foundation, Benevolence International Foundation, International Islamic Relief Organization, Muslim World League, Rabita Trust, and World Assembly of Muslim Youth.[82]

A Canadian intelligence assessment prepared on July 25, 2002, reported that individuals in Saudi Arabia "were donating 1 to 2 million a month through mosques and other fundraising avenues."[83] In August 2002, 600 family members of people who died on September 11, calling themselves "9/11 Families United to Bankrupt Terrorism," launched a $1 trillion lawsuit against parties that they allege have helped finance international terrorism. By March 2003, more than 3,100 plaintiffs had joined the lawsuit, whose list of terrorist financiers includes seven international banks, eight Islamic charities, several members of the Saudi Royal Family and the government of Sudan.[84] But class-action lawyer Ron Motley, the lead attorney in the case, said that the Bush administration was providing no help. After three meetings with State Department officials, he said, "we received zero pieces of paper and zero help."[85]

Saudi cooperation in the post-9/11 investigations was also lackluster. The *Boston Herald* reported in December 2001 that although terrorism suspects had been arrested in more than 40 countries following September 11, none had been announced in Saudi Arabia. The Saudis also balked at freezing the assets of organizations linked to bin Laden and international terrorism. The U.S. barely whispered about this lack of cooperation, for fear of disrupting what *Herald* reporters Jonathan Wells, Jack Meyers and Maggie Mulvihill described as "an extraordinary array of U.S.-Saudi business ventures which, taken together, are worth tens of billions of dollars."[86] They cited examples of top

Bush officials who have "cashed in on [the] Saudi gravy train," including the following:

- Vice President Dick Cheney's old company, Halliburton, has done more than $174 million in business developing oil fields and other projects for the Saudis.
- National Security Adviser Condoleezza Rice is a former longtime member of the board of directors of Chevron, which does extensive business with the Saudis. Rice even has a Chevron oil tanker named after her.
- The president's father, George H. W. Bush, works as a senior adviser to the Carlyle Group, which has financial interests in U.S. defense firms hired by the Saudis to equip and train their military.[87]

"It's good old-fashioned 'I'll scratch your back, you scratch mine.' You have former U.S. officials, former presidents, aides to the current president, a long line of people who are tight with the Saudis, people who are the pillars of American society and officialdom," said Charles Lewis of the Center for Public Integrity. "No one wants to alienate the Saudis, and we are willing to basically ignore inconvenient truths that might otherwise cause our blood to boil. We basically look away."[88]

The administration's ties to the Saudis through the Carlyle Group are especially intricate. Carlyle, an investment equity firm, is America's eleventh largest military contractor and one of the biggest "old boys networks" in the modern business world, bringing together high-powered former politicians with Saudi financial moguls and other major investors. The chairman of the Carlyle Group is Frank C. Carlucci, a former secretary of defense under Ronald Reagan and old college classmate of current defense secretary Donald Rumsfeld. Carlyle's other employees include a roster of former top-level government officials from the United States and other countries, including former British prime minister John Major, former U.S. secretary of state James A. Baker III, and former White House budget director Dick Darman. The former politicians work as rainmakers, using their reputations and contacts to help grease the wheels for weapons contracts and other high-stakes insider deals. "The revolving door has long been a fact of life in Washington, but Carlyle has given it a new spin," reported *Fortune* magazine in March 2002. "Instead of toiling away for a trade organization or consulting firm for a measly $250,000 a year, former government officials can rake in serious cash by getting equity cuts on corporate deals. Several of the onetime government officials who have hooked up with Carlyle—Carlucci, Baker, and Darman, in particular—have made millions."[89]

On March 5, 2001, Leslie Wayne of the *New York Times* reported that the elder George Bush had taken time off from campaigning for his son's presidential election "to call on Crown Prince Abdullah of Saudi Arabia at a luxurious desert compound outside Riyadh to talk about American-Saudi business affairs. Mr. Bush went as an ambassador of sorts, but not for his government. . . . Traveling with the fanfare of dignitaries, Mr. Bush and [former secretary of state James A. Baker III] were using their extensive government contacts to further their business interests as representatives of the Carlyle Group, a $12 billion private equity firm based in Washington that has parlayed a roster of former top-level government officials, largely from the Bush and Reagan administrations, into a moneymaking machine." Wayne noted that Bush Sr. was receiving $80,000 to $100,000 per speech for his activities on behalf of Carlyle and that the company had also helped Bush Jr. in 1990 by putting him on the board of a Carlyle subsidiary, Caterair, an airline-catering company.[90]

The strange bedfellows at Carlyle's slumber party included family members of Osama bin Laden, several of whom were in the United States doing business on the day of the September 11 attacks. Although the family has disowned him and publicly condemns his terrorist activities, the family's $2 million investment in Carlyle raised eyebrows. At the request of other shareholders, the bin Ladens sold their stake in Carlyle immediately after 9/11.[91] To handle PR aspects of the controversy regarding its links to the bin Ladens, the Carlyle Group hired Chris Ullman, a former official with the U.S. Office of Management and Budget, as its vice president for corporate communications.[92] The bin Ladens (who now spell their last name Binladin to differentiate themselves from Osama) went shopping for a public relations firm of their own, approaching Steven Goldstein and his PR firm, Attention America. Goldstein, who is Jewish and pro-Israel, came to the conclusion that he was approached in part because of his religious and political stance.[93] He turned them down, and the Binladins turned instead to the public relations firms of Hullin Metz & Co.[94] and WMC Communications, headed by former Hill & Knowlton chairman David Wynne-Morgan. "We have checked them out and they have no links with terrorism," Wynne-Morgan said.[95]

The Saudi monarchy also turned to public relations firms for assistance following September 11. Three days after the 9/11 attacks, the PR giant Burson-Marsteller signed an agreement to provide "issues counseling and crisis management" for the Kingdom and to place ads in the *New York Times* expressing Saudi support for the U.S. in its time of crisis.[96] In November, it began paying $200,000 per month to another PR firm, Qorvis Communications, and its affiliate, Patton Boggs. During the last nine months of 2002 alone, reported *O'Dwyer's PR Daily*, Qorvis received $20.2 million from the Kingdom. "That amount exceeds the previous record $14.2 million that the Citizens for a Free Kuwait front group spent at Hill & Knowlton during a six-month period in 1990–'91 to build support for the Persian Gulf War," *O'Dwyer's* reported. Qorvis helped the Saudis set up their own front group, called the Alliance for Peace and Justice, described in the PR firm's government filing as an American organization concerned about the Middle East process. Qorvis arranged media interviews for Saudi representatives with media figures including Ted Koppel, Bill Plant,

Paula Zahn, Andrea Mitchell, Aaron Brown, Chris Matthews and Bill O'Reilly."[97]

Hill & Knowlton also courted the Saudis, with H&K account manager Jim Cox giving an obsequious interview to *Arab News*, a publication owned by members of the monarchy. Described as "forthright and straight talking" by *Arab News*, Cox explained that "Saudi Arabia has a cadre of friends who know, respect and value it in terms of business relationships and the culture of the Kingdom. The trouble is that cadre is very small. It's a real industry-based group, limited to those who have had business contacts with the Kingdom." Due to the fact that the majority of the 9/11 hijackers were Saudis, Cox said, the Kingdom had "this huge hurdle of disbelief to overcome." But who's to blame? "It's not the Saudis, it's not the government, and it's not anybody else in particular. It's simply the world we live in."[98] Hill & Knowlton signed deals in excess of $77,000 per month with state-owned companies including Saudi Basic Industries and Saudi Aramco, the world's largest oil company.[99] Another PR firm, the Gallagher Group, headed by Republican policy analyst Jamie Gallagher, signed a $300,000, one-year deal in early 2003 to assist Qorvis Communications in its PR work for the Kingdom.[100]

Patton Boggs, a Qorvis affiliate, distributed documents to journalists and members of Congress portraying the Saudis as partners in the war on terror and victims themselves of terrorism.[101] One document addressed "hot button" issues such as "Saudi Support for Osama bin Laden," "Alleged Saudi Funding for Terrorism," "Saudi Freezing of Assets," "Saudi Education System and Anti-Americanism," "Saudi Arabia and Suicide Bombers," and "Stability in Saudi Arabia."[102] For the most part, however, the document stayed away from specifics on each of those points, preferring instead to rely on statements of endorsement for the Kingdom from U.S. officials including George W. Bush, Donald Rumsfeld, Pentagon spokesperson Torie Clarke, State Department spokesperson Richard Boucher, Colin Powell, White House press secretary Ari Fleischer and General Tommy Franks.[103]

Sometimes the Saudis were their own worst enemies in the PR war. In December 2001, for example, the Saudi defense minister drew criticism when he publicly accused the "Zionist and Jewish lobby" of orchestrating a "media blitz" against the desert kingdom.[104]

Just as American propaganda has limited impact in the Middle East, the Saudi PR blitz fell on mostly deaf ears in the United States. Millions of Saudi dollars went into TV and print ads positioning Saudi Arabia as a trusted ally of the U.S. and a partner in the war on terror.[105] "The ads are signed 'The People of Saudi Arabia,' but that's a lie," commented *Advertising Age* columnist Bob Garfield. "And so is the premise. For decades, the U.S. relationship with Saudi Arabia and other so-called 'moderate' Arab states has been a deal with the devil. We sponsor their corrupt, repressive, authoritarian regimes with cash and weaponry. They sell us oil. Such unholy alliances, dictated by Cold War *realpolitik*, were bound to create backlash, and so they have, in the 1979 Iranian revolution and decades of state-sponsored terrorism. In Saudi Arabia and Egypt, meanwhile, we have continued to deal with the devils we know rather than risk the Pandora's Box of popular Islamism. The results: A Saudi regime that pays protection money to radical fundamentalists by underwriting hate-spewing madrassas around the Muslim world, spreading the virus of radical Islam while inoculating itself from revolutionary threats within its kingdom."[106]

Although most of the flacks on retainer to the Saudis had Republican connections, some of the most scathing critics of the Kingdom were conservatives like *Wall Street Journal* columnist William McGurn and Congressman Dan Burton (R–Indiana), who held hearings in October 2002 on charges that American children born of mixed U.S./Saudi parents have been kidnapped to the Kingdom and held there. There are "hundreds of such cases," Burton said, adding that the U.S. State Department had done nothing to pressure the Kingdom to return American children held there against their will. U.S. reluctance to address the kidnapping matter made Burton wonder whether "we have the resolve to deal with Saudi Arabia on other issues, ranging from funding for terrorists to cooperation in the effort against Iraq."[107]

Qorvis helped the Saudis handle fallout from the charges, prompting Burton to subpoena the PR firm's records. When the Saudis claimed that this would violate diplomatic privileges under the Vienna Convention, Burton responded with a scathing letter, stating that the convention "has no application to

American citizens who choose to sell their services as public relations/lobbying mouthpieces for foreign interests. To the contrary, the Foreign Agents Registration Act, which was enacted by Congress in 1937, makes clear that the activities of such 'propagandists,' including the documents they generate, are to be subject to the 'spotlight of pitiless publicity' so that the American people may be fully informed of both the identity of the propagandists and the nature of the activities they undertake on behalf of their foreign masters."[108]

Even within Qorvis, the Saudi account seemed to stir concern. In December 2002, three of the company's founders quit to form their own PR firm. "Associates say their departure reflects a deep discomfort in representing the government of Saudi Arabia against accusations that Saudi leaders have turned a blind eye to terrorism," the *New York Times* reported on December 6, 2002. "Friends and associates, speaking on condition of anonymity, said the departures had been prompted largely by growing evidence of ties between prominent Saudis and the financing of the terrorism network Al Qaeda."[109]

4. Doublespeak

"**IN OUR TIME,** political speech and writing are largely the defense of the indefensible," George Orwell wrote in 1946. "Things like the continuance of British rule in India, the Russian purges and deportations, the dropping of the atom bombs on Japan, can indeed be defended, but only by arguments which are too brutal for most people to face, and which do not square with the professed aims of the political parties. Thus political language has to consist largely of euphemism, question-begging and sheer cloudy vagueness."[1]

Orwell was a shrewd observer of the relationship between

politics and language. He did not actually invent the term "doublespeak," but he popularized the concept, which is an amalgam of two terms that he coined in *1984*, his greatest novel. Orwell used the term "double*think*" to describe a contradictory way of thinking that lets people say things that mean the opposite of what they actually think. He used the term "*new*speak" to describe words "deliberately constructed for political purposes: words, that is to say, which not only had in every case a political implication, but were intended to impose a desirable mental attitude upon the person using them."[2]

For example, consider the now-famous phrase, "axis of evil," which was first used by President Bush in his January 29, 2002, State of the Union address. Bush characterized Iran, Iraq and North Korea as an "axis of evil, arming to threaten the peace of the world. By seeking weapons of mass destruction, these regimes pose a grave and growing danger. They could provide these arms to terrorists, giving them the means to match their hatred. They could attack our allies or attempt to blackmail the United States."[3]

The concept of an "axis," of course, evokes memories of the "Axis powers" of World War II and functions to prepare the public for acceptance of war against nations that purportedly belong to the axis. However, this use of the term is misleading. It suggests an alliance or confederation of states that pose a significant danger precisely because of their common alignment—a menace greater than the sum of the parts. In fact, Iran and Iraq have been bitter adversaries for decades, and there is no pattern of collaboration between North Korea and the other two states.

To say that these nations are "evil" depends in part on your theology and in part on your politics. There is no question that Iran, Iraq and North Korea have all committed horrible violations of human rights, although Iran has recently been undergoing internal democratization (a process that may be disrupted as the invasion of Iraq fans the flames of Islamic fundamentalism). The singling out of these particular nations as evil, however, invites the question of why the Bush administration failed to include U.S.-supported nations that violate human rights on a comparable scale, such as Colombia or Saudi Arabia, as well as countries that already possess nuclear weapons, such as China, France or Israel and Britain—not to mention India and Pakistan, which recently came close to using them. In reality, "axis of evil" is a term chosen to selectively stigmatize countries for the purpose of justifying military actions against them.

Bush's use of the term "axis of evil" sparked a number of jokes, such as a humorous news spoof on SatireWire.com. "Bitter after being snubbed for membership in the 'Axis of Evil,' Libya, China, and Syria today announced they had formed the 'Axis of Just as Evil,'" it stated. Also, "Cuba, Sudan, and Serbia said they had formed the 'Axis of Somewhat Evil,'" and "Bulgaria, Indonesia, and Russia established the 'Axis of Not So Much Evil Really As Just Generally Disagreeable.'"[4] Jokes notwithstanding, however, the term has played an influential role in creating the frame through which the public has perceived the problem of terrorism and the question of whether to go to war with Iraq.

Coalition of the Coerced

If the bad guys have an "axis," the good guys have a "coalition of the willing," to use the term preferred by Colin Powell and other U.S. officials and often repeated uncritically by major television news outlets, as we shall discuss later in chapter six, "The Air War." The word "coalition" attempted to evoke the feeling of international unity that existed in 1991, when the first Bush administration persuaded the United Nations to endorse a broad international coalition of nations that participated in the war to drive Iraq from Kuwait.

The Bush administration frequently compared the level and scope of international support for its military operations in Iraq to the coalition that fought the first Persian Gulf War. "The coalition against Iraq, called Operation Iraqi Freedom, is large and growing," stated Secretary of Defense Donald Rumsfeld at a press briefing on March 20, 2003. "This is not a unilateral action, as is being characterized in the media. Indeed, the coalition in this activity is larger than the coalition that existed during the Gulf War in 1991."[5] As the *Washington Post*'s Glenn Kessler pointed out, however, these statements were "exaggerations, according to independent experts and a review of figures from both conflicts."

The so-called "coalition of the willing" was almost entirely a
U.S.-British campaign, with virtually no military contribution
from any other country except Australia. "It's a baldfaced lie to
suggest that" the coalition for this war is greater than that for the
1991 war, said Ivo H. Daalder, a former Clinton administration
official who supported the war against Iraq. "Even our great allies Spain, Italy and Bulgaria are not providing troops."[6]

The nations that participated in the 1991 war but refused in
2003 included many of the leading nations of Europe, the
Middle East and other parts of the world: Bahrain, Egypt,
France, Germany, Greece, Morocco, Qatar, Saudi Arabia, and
the United Arab Emirates. In their place, the United States recruited countries such as Albania, Azerbaijan, the Dominican
Republic, El Salvador, Eritrea, Ethiopia, Kazakhstan, the Marshall Islands, Micronesia, Nicaragua, Palau (total population:
18,766), Rwanda, Uganda and Uzbekistan. By comparison
with the first Gulf War, very few of the nations in the 2003
coalition provided money or supplies or troops. Instead, they offered token support, such as political endorsements or permission to use their airspace for flyovers by U.S. warplanes. Rather
than *providing* material support, in fact, many nations sought
substantial financial aid packages or other U.S. support—such
as admission to NATO—in exchange for their endorsements.

By the date that war commenced, the United States had cob-
bled together a list of 30 nations that were willing to be publicly
named as supporting the war, and it claimed to have a list of
another 15 nations that secretly supported the war but wished

Controversy of conflict

to remain anonymous—described sarcastically by critics as "the coalition of the unwilling to be named." Even in the nations that *were* willing to be named in support of the war, the actual *people* of those nations mostly opposed it. According to a survey of the British population in January 2003, 68 percent remained unconvinced of the need for war. In Spain, 80 percent opposed the war, as did 73 percent in Italy, 79 percent in Denmark, 67 percent in the Czech Republic, 82 percent in Hungary and 63 percent in Poland.[7]

Noble Warriors

Doublespeak has accompanied war for thousands of years. English professor William Lutz has found examples as early as Julius Caesar, who described his brutal and bloody conquest of Gaul as "pacification." "The military is acutely aware that the reason for its existence is to wage war, and war means killing people and the deaths of American soldiers as well," he states. "Because the reality of war and its consequences are so harsh, the military almost instinctively turns to doublespeak when discussing war."[8] Doublespeak often suggests a noble cause to justify the death and destruction. Practically speaking, a democratic country cannot wage war without the popular support of its citizens. A well-constructed myth, broadcast through mass media, can deliver that support even when the noble cause itself seems dubious to the rest of the world.

The "code names" used to designate wars have also become part of the branding process through which war is made to seem noble. Rather than referring to the invasion of Panama as simply a war or invasion, it became "Operation Just Cause." (Note also the way that the innocuous word "operation" becomes part of the substitute terminology for war.) The war in Afghanistan was originally named "Operation Infinite Justice," a phrase that offended Muslims, who pointed out that only God can dispense infinite justice, so the military planners backed down a bit and called it "Operation Enduring Freedom" instead.[9] For the invasion of Iraq, they chose "Operation Iraqi Freedom." In *PR Week*, columnist Paul Holmes examined the significance of the term. "It's possible, I suppose, that Iraqi freedom might be a by-product of this campaign," he wrote, "but to pretend that it's what the exercise is all about is intellectual dishonesty at its most perverse."[10] However, the phrase served as a powerful framing device. Television networks including Fox and MSNBC used "Operation Iraqi Freedom" as their tag line for the war, with the phrase appearing in swooshing 3-D logos accompanied by imagery of flags and other symbols of patriotism. Other phrases favored by the Bush administration—"the disarmament of Iraq," "coalition forces," the "war on terror," "America strikes back"—appeared frequently in visual banners, graphics, and bottom-of-the-screen crawls, repeating and reinforcing the government's key talking points in support of war.

Cavalry to the Rescue

Sometimes language is chosen for its ability to avoid the plain meaning of what its writers are talking about. Numerous examples of this can be found in "Rebuilding America's Defenses: Strategies, Forces and Resources for a New Century," a report published in the year 2000 by the Project for the New American Century (PNAC), whose members, as described previously in chapter two, constitute much of the brain trust for the Bush administration's foreign policy. Criticized overseas as a blueprint for U.S. global domination, the report began by stating that the United States at present is a lone superpower that "faces no global rival. America's grand strategy should aim to preserve and extend this advantageous position as far into the future as possible." To achieve this goal, it recommended establishing permanent U.S. military bases in the Middle East and in regions of the world where they do not currently exist, including southeastern Europe, Latin America and Southeast Asia. It also said that the military should seek to "control the new 'international commons' of space and 'cyberspace,' and pave the way for the creation of a new military service—U.S. Space Forces—with the mission of space control." In addition, it spoke of the "need to develop a new family of nuclear weapons . . . safer and more effective nuclear weapons" that are "required in targeting the very deep, underground hardened bunkers that are being built by many of our potential adversaries."[11] Of course, these ideas sound a bit radical if stated too clearly, so PNAC needed to find language that would soften their meaning.

The PNAC report stated that the United States needs to "perform the 'constabulary' duties associated with shaping the security environment in critical regions." The phrase "constabulary duties" is a vague way of transforming U.S. soldiers occupying foreign countries into friendly neighborhood cops. "Shaping the security environment" is polite language for controlling other people at gunpoint, and "critical regions" is a nice way of saying "countries we want to control." Similarly, U.S. nuclear weapons—which would be called "weapons of mass destruction" if someone else owned them—are described as "the U.S. nuclear deterrent," while missiles with global reach are "defenses to defend the American homeland." How do they "defend" us? They "provide a secure basis for U.S. power projection around the world."

In deciphering phrases like this, it helps to pause periodically and try to imagine how these phrases must sound to people who do not live in the United States. To accomplish this, simply imagine that some country *other* than the United States—the former Soviet Union, Iraq, or for that matter Italy or India— were to issue a document that speaks of using missiles to "provide a secure basis for Italian power projection around the world" and "deter the rise of a new great-power competitor." Doublespeak enables PNAC to be simultaneously candid and ambiguous as it speaks of establishing "an American peace" that "must have a secure foundation on unquestioned U.S. military preeminence," in which U.S. troops are stationed throughout the world as the "first line of defense" of an "American security perimeter." Since the collapse of the Soviet empire, PNAC adds, "this perimeter has expanded slowly but inexorably. . . . In the decade since the end of the Cold War, the Persian Gulf and the surrounding region has witnessed a geometric increase in the presence of U.S. armed forces." If some *other* country were to "geometrically increase" the number of soldiers it deploys throughout the world, of course, we would see this as cause for alarm. Since these are *American* soldiers, however, they merely constitute a "cavalry on the new American frontier."

Here is how PNAC uses doublespeak to express the idea that this "cavalry" should become a permanent occupying army in the Middle East:

> From an American perspective, the value of such bases would endure even should Saddam pass from the scene. Over the long term, Iran may well prove as large a threat to U.S. interests in the Gulf as Iraq has. And even should U.S.-Iranian relations improve, retaining forward-based forces in the region would still be an essential element in U.S. security strategy given the longstanding American interests in the region.

Translated into plain English, this passage would say, "No matter what kind of government they have, we want our soldiers there so we can control their oil." However, there are taboos against speaking this frankly, so the writers speak instead of "forward-based forces" as a euphemism for soldiers and "longstanding American interests" as a euphemism for oil.[12]

Shocking and Awful

Sometimes doublespeak can *seem* very vivid and candid while nevertheless obscuring the real meaning of what is being discussed. For example, "shock and awe" was the term the Bush administration used to announce its strategy of massive, high-tech air strikes on Baghdad. As a doctrine of warfare, this term was introduced in a 1996 book by military strategists Harlan K. Ullman and James P. Wade and published by the Command and Control Research Program (CCRP) within the Office of the Assistant Secretary of Defense of the United States.[13] Titled *Shock and Awe: Achieving Rapid Dominance*, the book describes "shock and awe" as a strategy "aimed at influencing the will, perception, and understanding of an adversary rather than simply destroying military capability." It points to several examples in which this strategy has been successful in the past, including:

- **The dropping of atom bombs at Hiroshima and Nagasaki:** "The intent here is to impose a regime of Shock and Awe through delivery of instant, nearly incomprehensible levels of massive destruction directed at influencing society writ large, meaning its leadership and public, rather than targeting directly against military or strategic objectives even with relatively few numbers or systems," Ullman and Wade wrote.

- **The Nazi blitzkrieg strategy of World War II:** "In real Blitzkreig [sic], Shock and Awe were not achieved through the massive application of firepower across a broad front nor through the delivery of massive levels of force. Instead, the intent was to apply precise, surgical amounts of tightly focused force to achieve maximum leverage but with total economies of scale. . . . The lesson for future adversaries about the Blitzkreig [sic] example and the United States is that they will face in us an opponent able to employ technically superior forces with brilliance, speed, and vast leverage in achieving Shock and Awe through the precise application of force."

As these passages demonstrate—and as U.S. major Mark J. Conversino wrote in a 1998 book review published by the *Navy War College Review*—the text of *Shock and Awe* is "rambling, repetitious, and at times incoherent."[14] (This is to be expected, since, as Orwell observes, "The great enemy of clear language is insincerity. When there is a gap between one's real and one's declared aims, one turns as it were instinctively to long words and exhausted idioms, like a cuttlefish spurting out ink."[15]) Moreover, Conversino added, the "evidence used to support the concept of shock and awe is uneven. The authors make a strong case for Germany's blitzkrieg campaigns as an example of shock and awe, but sadly, the book's editors are obviously unfamiliar with that Wehrmacht strategy, consistently spelling the German word as 'blitzkreig.' . . . In an incomprehensible leap of logic, the Nazi Holocaust is classified a 'state policy of Shock and Awe.'"[16]

In January 2003, as the Bush administration moved toward war with Iraq, *Shock and Awe* author Harlan K. Ullman again invoked the example of Hiroshima as he explained the concept to CBS News. "You have this simultaneous effect, rather like the nuclear weapons at Hiroshima, not taking days or weeks but in minutes," he said. "You're sitting in Baghdad and all of a sudden you're the general and 30 of your division headquarters have been wiped out. You also take the city down. By that I mean you get rid of their power, water. In two, three, four, five days they are physically, emotionally and psychologically exhausted."[17]

Upon the onset of actual war, however, military and media pundits depicted "shock and awe" in sanitary terms, claiming that the high accuracy of laser-guided "smart bombs" would make it possible to decapitate the Iraqi military while leaving the country's infrastructure intact and limiting civilian casualties. Similar claims were made during the first war in the Persian Gulf and were later found to be exaggerated. Like other examples of doublespeak, the concept of "shock and awe" enables its users to symbolically reconcile two contradictory ideas.

On the one hand, its theorists use the term to plan massive uses of deadly force. On the other hand, its focus on the psychological *effect* of that force makes it possible to use the term while distancing audiences from direct contemplation of the human suffering which that force creates.

The Fog of War

Sometimes doublespeak completely reverses the meaning of words. Writing in *PR Week*, commentator Paul Holmes observed that "the most Orwellian usage of all has been the recent application of the word 'relevance,' as in 'the United Nations faced a test of its relevance, and failed.' Relevance, in this context, means willingness to rubberstamp whatever demands the US makes. If that sounds very much like irrelevance to you, perhaps you don't understand the might-makes-right world in which we are living."[18]

In normal times, "diplomacy" refers to the process by which nations seek to resolve their differences peacefully, through negotiations and compromise. During the buildup to war, however, "diplomacy" became the process through which the United States attempted to pressure other nations into supporting the war. When they refused, this became the "failure of diplomacy."

Similarly, the Bush administration used the phrase "preemptive defense" to describe its decision to attack first, without an overt act of Iraqi provocation—a phrase that could be used to justify attacking anyone we want on the grounds that they might attack us one day. Note also the substitution of the word "defense" for "war"—a perennial use of doublespeak that dates back in the United States to 1947, when the Department of War was renamed the "Department of Defense."[19]

Sometimes language merely fogs up the meaning of things. "Regime change," another phrase credited to the Project for the New American Century, sanitizes the imperial project of overthrowing a foreign government through a military invasion. It makes the process seem tidy, efficient and rational. The phrase makes it possible to talk about invading Iraq without even thinking about the human consequences: assassination, occupation or the deaths of thousands of innocents. And indeed there was little debate in the United States about these realities prior to the war. No questions were raised in the administration or Congress about whether the social cost actually justified the military action. Of course, raising such questions does not necessarily mean you must oppose military action. It is possible to raise these issues and to still argue that the benefits of invading Iraq and overthrowing its government outweigh the costs. In the United States, however, the Bush administration never attempted to make such an argument. Instead, it used language to sidestep addressing the harms caused by war.

The *Chicago Tribune*'s Bob Kemper reported that federal civilian employees and military personnel were told by the White House to refer to the invasion of Iraq as a "war of liberation." Iraqi paramilitary forces were to be called "death squads."[20]

The War to Never End Wars

The idea of a "war on terrorism" is itself a form of doublespeak. It reflects a now-pervasive habit of using war as a metaphor for all sorts of things that are not really wars at all. "Do you ever notice in this country that when we have a problem with something, we always have to declare *war* on it?" the comedian George Carlin once quipped. "The War on Illiteracy, the War on AIDS, the War on Homelessness, the War on Drugs . . . We don't actually *do* anything about it, but we've declared war on it."

The history of America's wars for higher purposes really begins with the First World War, which was sold to Americans as "the war to end war" and "the war to make the world safe for democracy." Today, nearly a century later, we can see how empty those slogans actually were. Usually, the people who launch metaphorical wars realize at the outset that victory, as understood in *real* wars, will never happen. Drug use, poverty, disease and terrorism have all existed for a very long time, and they're not going to disappear simply because some politician declares war against them. Instead, what usually happens is that these wars develop permanent bureaucracies that drain resources and issue periodic exhortations to the public as a way of compensating for the fact that victory is nowhere in sight.

At the very beginning of the "war on terrorism," a reporter asked Donald Rumsfeld, "Sir, what constitutes a victory in this new environment? I mean, Cap Weinberger in 1987 laid down some pretty clear rules for engaging U.S. forces. One was clear goals that are militarily achievable, that you can explain that there's an endgame. What's some of your early thinking here in terms of what constitutes victory?"

"That's a good question, as to what constitutes victory," Rumsfeld replied. "I would characterize it this way. I think that we're unlikely to be successful in changing the nature of human beings." Moreover, "Because of the end of the Cold War and because of the Gulf War, which told people not to compete with armies, navies and air forces, countries do look for asymmetrical ways they can threaten the United States and Western countries. With proliferation, with the relaxation of tension, that proliferation enables people to get their hands on capabilities that are increasingly powerful, powerful to the point that you're not talking about thousands, you're talking about multiples of thousands of people. . . . We have to recognize the magnitude of the threat and the extent to which people are willing to give their lives, as these pilots of these airplanes did, and impose damage on us."

The word "asymmetrical" in the passage above is a reference to "asymmetrical warfare," a term that military planners use to describe strategies such as terrorism. Asymmetrical warfare enables people with few military or economic resources to confront enemies who are much stronger than themselves. After thusly suggesting that U.S. imperial dominance is precisely the reason why suicide bombers are flying airplanes into our buildings, Rumsfeld finally got around to answering the question:

Ultimate focus of public perception
→) *Success of Iraqi invasion*

"Now, what is victory? I say that victory is persuading the American people and the rest of the world that this is not a quick matter that's going to be over in a month or a year or even five years. It is something that we need to do so that we can continue to live in a world with powerful weapons and with people who are willing to use those powerful weapons. And we can do that as a country. And that would be a victory, in my view."[21]

Rumsfeld is a clever man, and figuring out the meaning behind his words requires careful reading. At first glance, you might be tempted to think that he was saying that the United States would win a victory by maintaining its own possession of "powerful weapons." Actually, though, he was admitting that even as a superpower, the United States will not be able to stop the rest of the world from obtaining powerful weapons with which to "impose damage on us."

Therefore, if terrorism *itself* cannot be ended, Rumsfeld was saying, we need to change the way we think about the problem, so that we know better than to expect an "endgame" to the war on terror. His definition of victory, in short, becomes "persuading the American people" that real victory will never happen, and that the war itself may continue indefinitely.

President Bush explained the concept more succinctly in April 2003, after visiting wounded soldiers from the war in Iraq. "I reminded them and their families," he said, "that the war in Iraq is really about peace."[22]

Now *that's* doublespeak.

5. The Uses of Fear

BOTH TERROR AND PROPAGANDA have taken many forms throughout history, but terrorism as a *form of propaganda* has become one of the most destabilizing and dangerous phenomena afflicting modern society. Military campaigns have always sought to inspire fear in enemy soldiers as part of the battle for "hearts and minds." Most military campaigns, however, use fear as a secondary tactic within a war whose ultimate objective is seizing or destroying the enemy's territory, weapons, material resources and physical ability to wage war. Terrorism, by contrast, is a tactic often employed by political actors that have no hope of ever physically vanquishing their enemy. Instead, their goal is to defeat the enemy *psychologically* through the systematic, calculated use of violence and threats of violence.

During the period from the 1870s to the 1920s, terrorism was sometimes associated with the political philosophy of anarchism, whose followers carried out a number of assassinations on corporate and government leaders, including U.S. president William McKinley. This strategy was described by nineteenth-century anarchist Mikhail Bakunin as "propaganda of the deed." The advocates of "propaganda of the deed" believed that the heroic, exemplary boldness of their actions would inspire the masses and make anarchist ideas famous. Unlike modern terrorists, however, they tended to target individuals whom they regarded as responsible for oppressing the masses, while avoiding violence against innocent bystanders. For example, Russian radicals intent on assassinating Tsar Alexander II in the mid-nineteenth century cancelled several actions out of concern that they might injure women, children or elderly persons.[1]

During the twentieth century, terrorism gradually evolved, becoming more deadly and indiscriminate as its practitioners sought to maximize the psychological impact of their actions. According to Jerrold Post, director of the Political Psychology Program at George Washington University, sophisticated terrorist groups actually study and use media relations and give out handbooks explaining how to attract maximum media attention. Speaking at the U.S. National Press Club on February

12, 2003, Post detailed a study showing that terrorist attacks in Northern Ireland tended to occur on Thursday afternoons between 5:00 and 6:00. "The reason is the deadline for Friday papers, that traditionally carry supermarket coupons and sales ads, is 6:00 p.m.," explained *O'Dwyer's PR Daily*, which covered Post's talk. "Any terrorist act committed before 5:00 p.m. would give journalists time to analyze the act and report it in context. After 5:00 p.m. all there's time to do is rip the current headline and put in the terrifying headline that the terrorists want to be seen, said Post."

Hafez Al Mirazi, bureau chief of the Al Jazeera satellite TV network, spoke at the same event as Post and agreed that terrorists exploit the media for maximum advantage. "If CNN or Fox or others are not going to have breaking news flashing on their screens if Palestinians are killed, but only if Israelis are killed, then [terrorists] will go out and kill an Israeli," Al Mirazi said.[2]

James E. Lukaszewski, a public relations counselor who advises the U.S. military and major corporations, goes further, stating that "media coverage and terrorism are soul mates— virtually inseparable. They feed off each other. They together create a dance of death—the one for political or ideological motives, the other for commercial success." Terrorists need the media to gain attention for their cause, and the sensational nature of their crimes drives up media ratings. "Terrorist activities are high profile, ratings-building events," Lukaszewski writes. "The news media need to prolong these stories because they build viewership and readership. . . . The marriage between the terrorist and the media is inevitable. It's a grizzly, predictable, often necessary dance of death."[3]

Lukaszewski made those observations in 1987, 14 years before Al Qaeda's attack on the Pentagon and the World Trade Center. They may seem extreme, and they would certainly draw objections from reporters like Dan Rather, who were as shocked and horrified by the events of that day as anyone else — perhaps more so, because they witnessed the events personally and watched even more footage than their TV audience. For that matter, Lukaszewski himself would probably take offense at the notion that he also has anything in common with terrorists. But what mass media, public relations, advertising and terrorism all have in common is a one-sided approach to communications that can best be thought of as a "propaganda model."

The propaganda model differs in many important respects from the assumptions about communication that we expect in a democracy. The differences begin with the very way that communication itself is defined. Propagandists view communications as a set of techniques for indoctrinating a "target audience," whereas the democratic concept of communication defines it as an ongoing process of dialogue among diverse voices. Of course, the propaganda approach becomes more attractive during wartime, when each side becomes preoccupied with manipulating and coercing the thinking of their enemy or domestic populations. "The propagandist wants to promote his or her own interests or those of an organization — sometimes at the expense of the recipients, sometimes not," write Garth Jowett and Victoria O'Donnell in their book, *Propaganda and Persuasion*. "The point is that the propagandist does not regard the well-being of the audience as a primary concern."[4] Propagandists also tend to have a low regard for the rationality and intelligence of their audience. In *Mein Kampf*, Adolf Hitler wrote that he preferred to speak before audiences that had just eaten dinner, when they were relaxed and sleepy. Early scholars who studied propaganda called it a "hypodermic needle approach" to communication, in which the communicator's objective was to "inject" his ideas into the minds of the target population.[5]

If this is your goal, an audience that thinks critically and is prepared to challenge your message becomes a problem that must be overcome. Whereas democracy is built upon the assumption that "the people" are capable of rational self-governance, propagandists regard rationality as an obstacle to efficient indoctrination. Since propaganda is often aimed at persuading people to do things that are not in their own best interests, it frequently seeks to bypass the rational brain altogether and manipulate us on a more primitive level, appealing to emotional symbolism. Advertisers speak of selling "the sizzle, not the steak." They plant bikini-clad women next to automobiles and beer mugs in the expectation that we will associate their products with sex. Television uses sudden, loud noises to provoke a startle response, bright colors, violence—not because these things are inherently appealing but because they catch our attention and keep us watching. When these practices are criticized, advertisers and TV executives respond that they do this because this is what their "audience wants." In fact, however, they are appealing selectively to certain aspects of human nature—the most primitive aspects, because those are the most predictable.

Fear is one of the most primitive emotions in the human psyche, and it definitely keeps us watching. If the mere ability to keep people watching were really synonymous with "giving audiences what they want," we would have to conclude that people "want" terrorism. On September 11, Osama bin Laden kept the entire world watching. As much as people hated what they were seeing, the power of their emotions kept them from turning away.

And fear can make people do other things that they would not do if they were thinking rationally. During the war crimes trials at Nuremberg, psychologist Gustave Gilbert visited Nazi Reichsmarshall Hermann Goering in his prison cell. "We got around to the subject of war again and I said that, contrary to his attitude, I did not think that the common people are very thankful for leaders who bring them war and destruction," Gilbert wrote in his journal, *Nuremberg Diary*.

"Why, of course, the *people* don't want war," Goering shrugged. "Why would some poor slob on a farm want to risk his life in a war when the best that he can get out of it is to come back to his farm in one piece? Naturally, the common people don't want war; neither in Russia nor in England nor in America, nor for that matter in Germany. That is understood. But, after all, it is the *leaders* of the country who determine the policy and it is always a simple matter to drag the people along, whether it is a democracy or a fascist dictatorship or a Parliament or a Communist dictatorship."

"There is one difference," Gilbert pointed out. "In a democracy the people have some say in the matter through their elected representatives, and in the United States only Congress can declare wars."

"Oh, that is all well and good," Goering responded, "but, voice or no voice, the people can always be brought to the bidding of the leaders. That is easy. All you have to do is tell them they are being attacked and denounce the pacifists for lack of patriotism and exposing the country to danger. It works the same way in any country."[6]

Arnold Gets a Hummer

Politicians and terrorists are not the only propagandists who use fear to drive human behavior in irrational directions. A striking recent use of fear psychology in marketing occurred following Operation Desert Storm in 1991. During the war, television coverage of armored Humvees sweeping across the desert helped launch the Hummer, a consumer version of a vehicle that was originally designed exclusively for military use. The initial idea

to make a consumer version came from actor Arnold Schwarz-
enegger, who wanted a tough-looking, road-warrior vehicle for
himself. At his prodding, AM General (what was left of the old
American Motors) began making civilian Hummers in 1992,
with the first vehicle off the assembly line going to Schwarz-
enegger himself.[7]

In addition to the Hummer, the war helped launch a broader
sport-utility vehicle craze in the United States. Psychiatrist Clo-
taire Rapaille, a consultant to the automobile industry, conducted studies of post-war consumer psyches for Chrysler and
reported that Americans wanted "aggressive" cars.[8] In interviews
with Keith Bradsher, the former Detroit bureau chief for the
New York Times, Rapaille candidly discussed the results of his
research. SUVs, he said, are "weapons"—"armored cars for the
battlefield"—that appeal to Americans' deepest fears of violence and crime.[9] Rapaille also helped plan Chrysler's PT
Cruiser, which was consciously designed to look like a gangster
car of the 1930s. It was designed, he said, to make drivers feel
like "Al Capone at the wheel, with a machine gun." The Dodge
Durango was designed to look like a savage jungle cat. "A
strong animal has a big jaw, that's why we put big fenders,"
Rapaille said.[10] Another hostility-intensification feature is the
"grill guard" that SUV manufacturers promote. "Grill guards,
useful mainly for pushing oryx out of the road in Namibia,
have no application under normal driving conditions," observes
writer Gregg Easterbrook. "But they make SUVs look angrier,
especially when viewed through a rearview mirror. . . . Grill

guards also increase the chance that an SUV will kill someone in an accident."[11]

Deliberately marketed as "urban assault luxury vehicles,"[12] SUVs exploit fear while actually doing nothing to make people safer. They make their owners feel safe, not by protecting them, but by feeding their aggressive impulses. Due to SUVs' propensity for rollovers, Bradsher notes, the occupant death rate in SUVs is actually 6 percent *higher* than for cars—8 percent higher in the largest SUVs.[13] Rapaille himself understands this very well; he refuses to drive an SUV, owing to the increased danger of rollovers.[14] Of course, they also get worse gas mileage. According to dealers, Hummers average a mere 8 to 10 miles per gallon[15]—a figure that takes on additional significance in light of the role that dependency on foreign oil has played in shaping U.S. relations with countries in the Middle East.

With this combination of features, selling SUVs on their merits would be a challenge, which is why Rapaille consistently advises Detroit to rely instead on irrational fear appeals. Six months after the 9/11 terrorist attacks, *Fortune* magazine reported that Ford Motors had joined Chrysler in seeking Rapaille's advice. Now that "the homeland is at war," Rapaille told them, automakers should use the themes of "safety and security" to sell vehicles. Moreover, he says, they should tailor their pitches to appeal to customers' most primitive emotions—what he called their "reptilian hot buttons." Some companies, he complained, still hadn't gotten with the program. "They are still producing cortex cars," he said.[16] By "cortex cars," of course, he was referring to vehicles whose owners make their purchase decisions based on a rational evaluation of features such as fuel-efficiency, safety and reliability.

War with Iraq in March 2003 also provided a boost to SUV sales, and to Hummers in particular. In fact, noted *New York Times* reporter Danny Hakim, the Hummer "continues to be the only Detroit brand that sells without incentives." In addition to the vehicle itself, the carmaker also did a brisk trade in Hummer "gear"—items like a $449 remote-controlled miniature Hummer equipped with spy camera and monitor, or a $795 Hummer Tactical Mountain Bike, patterned after foldable bicycles made for military paratroopers.[17]

"When I turn on the TV, I see wall-to-wall Humvees, and I'm proud," said Sam Bernstein, a 51-year-old antiquities dealer in California who drives a Hummer H2. "If I could get an Al Abrams [tank], I would."[18]

In addition to motor vehicles, other products and causes also exploited fear-based marketing following September 11. "The trick in 2002, say public affairs and budget experts, will be to redefine your pet issue or product as a matter of homeland security," wrote *PR Week*. "If you can convince Congress that your company's widget will strengthen America's borders, or that funding your client's pet project will make America less dependent on foreign resources, you just might be able to get what you're looking for."[19]

Alaska senator Frank Murkowski used fear of terrorism to press for federal approval of oil drilling in the Arctic National

Wildlife Refuge, telling his colleagues that U.S. purchases of foreign oil help subsidize Saddam Hussein and Palestinian suicide bombers.[20] The nuclear power industry lobbied for approval of Yucca Mountain, Nevada, as a repository for high-level radioactive waste by claiming that shipping the waste there would keep nuclear weapons material from falling into the hands of terrorists.[21] Of course, they didn't propose actually shutting down nuclear power plants, which themselves are prime targets for terrorists. According to the Associated Press, "A direct hit of a nuclear plant by a modern jumbo jet traveling at high speed 'could create a Chernobyl situation,' said a U.S. official who declined to be identified."[22] To counter this sort of concern among lawmakers, the Nuclear Energy Institute ran an advertisement in the January 26, 2002, *National Journal*, highlighting the "highly committed, highly trained . . . expert marksmen" who stand guard at nuclear power plants, ready to fend off any threat that might come their way.[23] (Of course, even a "highly trained" marksman would not be able to shoot down an incoming 747.)

The National Drug Council retooled the war on drugs with television advertisements telling people that smoking marijuana helped fund terrorism. Environmentalists attempted to take the fund-a-terrorist trope in a different direction, teaming up with columnist Arianna Huffington to launch the "Detroit Project," which produced TV ads modeled after the National Drug Council advertisements. "This is George," a voice-over said. "This is the gas that George bought for his SUV." The screen then showed a map of the Middle East. "These are the countries where the executives bought the oil that made the gas that George bought for his SUV." The picture switched to a scene of armed terrorists in a desert. "And these are the terrorists who get money from those countries every time George fills up his SUV." In Detroit and elsewhere, however, TV stations that had been only too happy to run the White House anti-drug ads refused to accept the Detroit Project commercials, calling them "totally inappropriate."[24]

September 11 was frequently compared to the Japanese attack on Pearl Harbor, with White House officials warning that the war on terror would be prolonged and difficult like World War II and would require similar sacrifices. Whatever those sacrifices may entail, however, almost from the start it was clear that they would not include frugality. During World War II, Americans conserved resources as never before. Rationing was imposed on gasoline, tires and even food. People collected waste such as paper and household cooking scraps so that it could be recycled and used for the war effort. Compare that to the headline that ran in *O'Dwyer's PR Daily* on September 24, less than two weeks after the terrorist attack: "PR Needed to Keep Consumers Spending." The article cited marketing and PR executive Maureen Lippe's opinion that the "greatest service PR pros can provide in support of the country is to ensure that the consumer continues to buy."[25]

President Bush himself appeared in TV commercials, urging Americans to "live their lives" by going ahead with plans for vacations and other consumer purchases. "The president of the United States is encouraging us to buy," wrote marketer Chuck Kelly in an editorial for the Minneapolis/St. Paul *Star Tribune*, which argued that America is "embarking on a journey of spiritual patriotism" that "is about pride, loyalty, caring and believing"—and, of course, selling. "Marketers of products and services must understand the complexities of spiritual patriotism to thrive in today's marketplace," he wrote. "As marketers, we have the responsibility to keep the economy rolling. . . . Our job is to create customers during one of the more difficult times in our history."[26]

Hail to the Chief

Fear also provided the basis for much of the Bush administration's surging popularity following September 11. In the week immediately prior to the terrorist attacks, Bush's standing in opinion polls was at its lowest point ever, with only 50 percent of respondents giving him a positive rating. Within two days of the attack, that number shot up to 82 percent.[27] Since then, whenever the public's attention has begun to shift away from topics such as war and terrorism, Bush has seen his domestic popularity ratings slip downward, spiking up again when war talk fills the airwaves. By March 13–14, 2003, his popularity had fallen to 53 percent—essentially where he stood with the public prior to 9/11. On March 18, Bush declared war with

Iraq, and ratings shot up again to 68 percent—even when, briefly, it appeared that the war might be going badly.[28]

"For the most part, Americans tend to rally around their president at stratospheric levels not so much as a reward for accomplishment or success but out of a perceived need for national unity—a coming together—in time of crisis," observes Ron Faucheaux, who edits *Campaigns & Elections* magazine, a trade publication for political campaign advisers. Only four presidents other than Bush have seen their job rating meet or surpass the 80 percent mark:

- Franklin Delano Roosevelt reached his highest rating ever—84 percent—immediately after the Japanese attacked Pearl Harbor.
- Harry Truman hit 87 percent right after FDR died during the final, crucial phase of World War II.
- John F. Kennedy hit 83 percent right after the failed Bay of Pigs invasion of Cuba, an episode that marked a colossal failure of U.S. policy by any possible interpretation.
- Dubya's dad, President George H. W. Bush, hit 89 percent during Operation Desert Storm.[29]

Other presidents have also seen their standings rise during moments of crisis, even when the nature of the crisis called the quality of their leadership into question. Nixon's highest rating came in 1969, after a week of intense protests against the Vietnam War. Reagan's popularity peaked when he was shot by

John Hinckley. Bill Clinton's highest rating came right after he was impeached by the House of Representatives following the Monica Lewinsky scandal.[30]

The War at Home

It seems to be a law of history that times of war and national fear are accompanied by rollbacks of civil liberties and attacks on dissent. During the Civil War, Abraham Lincoln suspended the right of habeas corpus. The Second World War brought the internment of Japanese-Americans, and the Cold War brought McCarthyism. On a global scale, these examples pale compared to the uses of fear to justify mass killings, torture and political arrests in countries such as Mao's China, Stalin's Russia or Saddam Hussein's Iraq. Nevertheless, these episodes have been dark moments in America's history.[31]

Although the Bush administration took pains to insist that "Muslims are not the enemy"[32] and that it viewed Islam as a "religion of peace,"[33] it was unable to prevent a series of verbal attacks against Muslims that have occurred in the United States following 9/11 — with some of the attacks coming from Bush's strongest supporters in the conservative movement. "This is no time to be precious about locating the exact individuals directly involved in this particular terrorist attack," wrote columnist Ann Coulter two days after the attacks. "We should invade their countries, kill their leaders and convert them to Christianity.

We weren't punctilious about locating and punishing only Hitler and his top officers. We carpet-bombed German cities; we killed civilians. That's war. And this is war."[34]

Of course, Coulter's column does not reflect the mainstream of American opinion. Even the conservative *National Review*, which published her column, later called it a "mistake" and ended its relationship with her.[35] However, it offers a telling illustration of the way that fear can drive people to say and do things that make them *feel* brave and powerful while actually making them less safe by fanning the flames of intolerance and violence. Rhetoric of this sort can be used interchangeably to ignite the worst fears and passions on both sides of a conflict. Shortly after Coulter's column appeared, it resurfaced on the website of the Mujahideen Lashkar-e-Taiba—one of the largest militant Islamist groups in Pakistan—which works closely with Al Qaeda. Visiting the Lashkar-e-Taiba site can be a bracing experience. During the period when Coulter's article was featured, the site was decorated with an image that depicted a hairy, monstrous hand with claws in place of fingernails, from which blood dripped onto a burning globe of planet Earth. A star of David decorated the wrist of the hairy hand, and behind it stood an American flag. The reproduction of Coulter's column used bold, red letters to highlight the sentence that said to "invade their countries, kill their leaders and convert them to Christianity." To make the point even stronger, the webmaster added a comment: "We told you so. Is anyone listening out there? The noose is already around our necks. The preparation for genocide of ALL Muslims has begun. . . . The media is now doing its ground work to create more hostility towards Islam and Muslims to the point that no one will oppose this mass murder which is about to take place. Mosques will be shut down, schools will be closed, Muslims will be arrested, and executed. There may even be special awards set up to kill Muslims. Millions and millions will be slaughtered like sheep. Remember these words because it is coming. The only safe refuge you have is Allah."[36]

Back on the other side of the divide, President Bush was compelled to issue a statement during the Islamic holy month of Ramadan in 2002, disavowing anti-Islamic comments by prominent conservative Christian leaders. Pat Robertson declared that Muslims were "worse than the Nazis" because "what the Muslims want to do to the Jews is worse."[37] A February 15, 2003, conference of the Christian Coalition of America (CCA) included speakers such as Daniel Pipes, who believes "increased stature, and affluence, and enfranchisement of American Muslims . . . will present true dangers to American Jews."[38] Another speaker at the CCA forum, syndicated columnist Don Feder, characterized Islam as a religion that, "throughout its 1,400-year history, has lent itself well to fanaticism, terrorism, mass murder, oppression and conversion by the sword."[39] Although the Bush administration has tried to distance itself from this sort of thing, it hasn't tried hard enough. That same month, Vice President Dick Cheney was a keynote speaker at the annual meeting of the Conservative Political Action Committee

(CPAC), where vendors at exhibition booths sold Islamiphobic paraphernalia such as a bumper sticker that said, "No Muslims—No Terrorism."[40]

Muslims have not been the only targets of politically motivated efforts to exploit public fears of terrorism. After John Walker Lindh, an American citizen, was captured fighting with the Taliban in Afghanistan, Ann Coulter attempted to link his decision to become a Muslim fundamentalist to his upbringing in liberal Marin County, California. "We need to execute people like John Walker in order to physically intimidate liberals, by making them realize that they can be killed too. Otherwise, they will turn out to be outright traitors," Coulter fumed before an audience of 3,500 people at the 2002 CPAC conference. Appearing on *Fox News* a few days later, she bragged that her comments had been a "huge hit with the audience."[41]

Corporate spin doctors, think tanks and conservative politicians have taken up the rhetoric of fear for their own purposes. Even before 9/11, many of them were engaged in an ongoing effort to demonize environmentalists and other activist groups by associating them with terrorism. One striking indicator of this preoccupation is the fact that Congressman Scott McInnis (R–Colorado) had scheduled congressional hearings on "ecoterrorism" to be held on September 12, 2001, one day after Congress itself was nearly destroyed in an attack by *real* terrorists. (The September 11 attacks forced McInnis to temporarily postpone his plans, rescheduling his hearings to February 2002.)[42]

In the immediate aftermath of 9/11, Republican congressman Don Young of Alaska speculated publicly that environmental extremists might be the real masterminds of the attacks.[43] On the Reagan Information Interchange, a website run by Ronald Reagan's son Michael, columnist Mary Mostert speculated that the culprits were probably "other Americans"— specifically, "environmentalist and anti-globalist groups . . . the radicals on the left."[44] Even after it became clear that Islamist fundamentalists were behind the attacks on the World Trade Center and the Pentagon, conservative attacks continued. On October 7, 2001, the *Washington Times* published an editorial calling for "war against eco-terrorists," calling them "an eco-al-Qaeda" with "a fanatical ideology and a twisted morality."[45]

Conservatives sometimes used the war on terrorism to demonize Democrats. Democratic Senate majority leader Tom Daschle was targeted by American Renewal, the lobbying wing of the Family Research Council, a conservative think tank that spends most of its time promoting prayer in public schools and opposing gay rights. In newspaper advertisements, American Renewal attempted to paint Daschle and Saddam Hussein as "strange bedfellows."[46] "What do Saddam Hussein and Senate Majority Leader Tom Daschle have in common?" stated a news release announcing the ad campaign. "Neither man wants America to drill for oil in Alaska's Arctic National Wildlife Refuge."[47]

William Bennett, Reagan's former education secretary, authored a book titled *Why We Fight: Moral Clarity and the War on Terrorism*. Through his organization, Empower America, he launched "Americans for Victory over Terrorism," a group of well-connected Republicans including Jack Kemp, Jeane Kirkpatrick and Trent Lott. "The threats we face today are both external and internal: external in that there are groups and states that want to attack the United States; internal in that there are those who are attempting to use this opportunity to promulgate their agenda of 'blame America first.' Both threats stem from either a hatred for the American ideals of freedom and equality or a misunderstanding of those ideals and their practice," he stated.[48]

In May 2002, controversy erupted when the Bush administration was forced to admit that it had received a general warning of possible airplane hijackings by terrorists prior to September 11.[49] Conservative pundits and politicians fought back by questioning the patriotism of critics. Democrats "need to be very cautious not to seek political advantage by making incendiary suggestions," said Vice President Dick Cheney (without specifying any "incendiary suggestions" that any Democrats had actually made).[50] On *Fox News*, conservative commentator Fred Barnes said that Democrats "looked like not a loyal opposition but a disloyal opposition, encouraging . . . conspiracy theories about how President Bush might have known about the terrorist attacks prior to September 11 and didn't do anything about them."[51] White House communications director Dan Bartlett told the *Washington Post* that Democrats are doing "exactly what our opponents, our enemies, want us to do."[52]

Washington Times reporter Ellen Sorokin used terrorist-baiting to attack the National Education Association, America's largest teachers' union and a frequent opponent of Republican educational policies. The NEA's crime was to create a "Remember September 11" website for use as a teaching aid on the first anniversary of the attack. The NEA site had a red-white-and-blue color motif, with links to the CIA and to Homeland Security websites, and it featured three speeches by President Bush, whom it described as a "great American." In order to make the case that the NEA was somehow anti-American, Sorokin hunted about on the site and found a link to an essay preaching tolerance toward Arab- and Muslim-Americans. "Everyone wants the terrorists punished," the essay wrote, but "we must not act like [the terrorists] by lashing out at innocent people around us, or 'hating' them because of their origins. . . . Groups of people should not be judged by the actions of a few. It is wrong to condemn an entire group of people by association with religion, race, homeland, or even proximity."

In a rather stunning display of intellectual dishonesty, Sorokin took a single phrase in the essay—"Do not suggest any group is responsible" (referring to Arab-Americans in general) and quoted it out of context to suggest that the NEA opposed holding the *terrorists* responsible for their deeds. Headlined "NEA delivers history lesson: Tells teachers not to cast 9/11 blame," her story went on to claim that the NEA simultaneously "takes a decidedly blame-America approach."[53] This in turn became the basis for a withering barrage of attacks as the right-wing media echo chamber, including TV, newspapers, talk radio and websites, amplified the accusation, complaining of "Terrorism in the Classroom"[54] as "Educators Blame America and Embrace Islam."[55] In the *Washington Post*, columnist George Will wrote that the NEA website "is as frightening, in its way, as any foreign threat."[56]

Patriot Games

If, as George Will insinuated, even schoolteachers are as scary as Saddam or Osama, no wonder the government needs to step in and crack the whip. Since 9/11, laws have been passed that place new limits on citizen rights, while expanding the government's authority to spy on citizens.

In October 2001, Congress passed the ambitiously named *USA Patriot Act*, which stands for "Uniting and Strengthening America by Providing Appropriate Tools Required to Intercept and Obstruct Terrorism." In addition to authorizing unprecedented levels of surveillance and incarceration of both citizens and non-citizens, the *USA Patriot Act* included provisions that explicitly target people simply for engaging in classes of political speech that are expressly protected by the U.S. Constitution. It expanded the ability of police to spy on telephone and Internet correspondence in anti-terrorism investigations and in routine criminal investigations unrelated to terrorism. It authorized *secret* government searches, enabling the FBI and other government agencies to conduct searches without warrants and without notifying individuals that their property has been searched. It created a broad new definition of "domestic terrorism" under which political protesters can be charged as terrorists if they engage in conduct that "involves acts dangerous to human life." It also put the CIA back in the business of spying on American citizens and allowed the government to detain non-citizens for indefinite periods of time without trial.[57] The *Patriot Act* was followed in November 2001 by a new executive order from President Bush, authorizing himself to order a trial in a military court for any non-citizen he designates, without a right of appeal or the protection of the Bill of Rights.[58]

"Mr. Bush has authorized military justice as an option for the government in a far wider array of cases than could ever be necessary," editorialized the *Washington Post*. "Any non-citizen whom the president deems to be a member of al Qaeda, or to be engaged in international terrorism of virtually any kind, or even to be harboring such people, can be detained indefinitely under his order and tried. The trials could take place using largely secret evidence. Depending solely on how the Defense Department further refines the rules, the military officers conducting the trials might insist on proof of guilt beyond a reasonable doubt, or might use some far lesser standard. The accused can be convicted without a unanimous verdict but with a two-thirds majority. Those found guilty would have no appeal to any court; and if found guilty, they could be executed. Such a process is only a hair's breadth from a policy of summary justice. The potential to imprison or execute many innocent people is large, the chances that such erosion would become known much smaller."[59]

The assault on individual rights continued in 2002 with a Pentagon project called "Total Information Awareness," masterminded by John Poindexter of Iran-Contra fame.[60] Poindexter envisioned creating a vast, centralized computer database that would pull together information about people from both commercial and government sources—everything from credit card purchases, magazine subscriptions and Internet activities to passport applications, driver's license, school, judicial and divorce records, and complaints from nosy neighbors. For once, opposition in Congress succeeded in killing the plan—on paper, at least. In May 2003, the Pentagon reported that it was going ahead with the plan, with one little difference—a name change from "Total Information Awareness" to "Terrorism Information Awareness."[61]

As if determined to prove that irony is not dead, the Ad Council launched a new series of public service advertisements, calling them a "Freedom Campaign," in July 2002. "What if America wasn't America? Freedom. Appreciate it. Cherish it. Protect it," read the tag line at the end of each TV ad, which attempted to celebrate freedom by depicting what America would look like without it. In one ad, a young man approaches a librarian with a question about a book he can't find. She tells him ominously that the book is no longer available, and the young man is taken away for questioning by a couple of government goons. The irony is that the USA *Patriot Act* had already empowered the FBI to seize book sales and library checkout records, while barring booksellers and librarians from saying anything about it to their patrons. It would be nice to imagine that someone at the Ad Council was trying to make a point in opposition to these encroachments on our freedoms. No such point was intended, according to Phil Dusenberry, who directed the ads. Interviewed on National Public Radio by Brooke Gladstone, Dusenberry sighed audibly when Gladstone mentioned the *Patriot Act*. "Our commercial and what you just described are purely a coincidence," he said. "The advertising can only go so far. . . . It can't really cross any line into, you know, anything that's more concrete."[62]

If We Tell You, Terrorists Will Kill You

Just as fear provides a rationale for the government to collect more information on its citizens, it also provides a pretext for withholding information from citizens who want to know what the government is doing.

In October 2001, U.S. attorney general John Ashcroft issued a new statement of policy that changes the way federal agencies respond to *Freedom of Information Act* (FOIA) requests. The Ashcroft declaration replaced a 1993 memorandum from Attorney General Janet Reno that created a "presumption of disclosure," ordering agencies to comply with such requests except when it was "reasonably foreseeable that disclosure would be harmful."[63] The new Ashcroft doctrine rejected this "foresee-able harm" standard and instructed agencies to withhold information whenever there was a "sound legal basis" for doing so. "When you carefully consider FOIA requests and decide to withhold records, in whole or in part, you can be assured that the Department of Justice will defend your decisions unless they lack a sound legal basis or present an unwarranted risk of adverse impact on the ability of other agencies to protect other important records," Ashcroft stated.[64]

"As with many of the Bush Administration's new restrictions on public information, the new policy is only peripherally related to the fight against terrorism," noted *Secrecy News*, a publication of the Federation of American Scientists. "Rather, it appears to exploit the current circumstances to advance a predisposition toward official secrecy."[65]

Corporations also lobbied for new rules limiting their obligations to release information. The American Chemistry Council (formerly known as the Chemical Manufacturers Association) made the threat of terrorism the centerpiece of its own newly aggressive campaign to roll back "public right-to-know" policies that enable citizens to learn about toxic hazards in their communities. Shortly after September 11, the *National Review* published an article by Jonathan Adler of the Competitive Enterprise Institute (CEI), calling on federal agencies to reconsider provisions of the *Clean Air Act* that require companies to prepare risk-management plans that detail potential chemical accidents and worst-case scenarios for what could happen to neighboring communities. By law, this information must be made available to the public—a practice that Adler described as "helping terrorists."[66] Such laws "actually promise to do more harm than good," stated a separate CEI editorial. "This information is only useful to groups that want to scare the public about chemical risks, or those who might use it for selecting targets."[67]

"Groups that want to scare the public" is a deft reference to environmental groups, which "scare the public" whenever they inform people that the chemical plant in their neighborhood is capable of emitting toxic plumes. CEI's argument is based on the subtle insinuation that this kind of "scaring" is itself akin to terrorism, an argument that corporate-funded think tanks have been making for years. It is also a paradoxical argument, since it is itself an argument based on fear, which attempts to "scare the public" about their own right to know. In essence, it says that people are safer not knowing about things that might hurt them. And like many fear-based arguments, it does not hold up to rational scrutiny.

The attempt to link right-to-know with terrorism has been ongoing since 1998, when the American Chemistry Council hired former security agency personnel to write a report titled "The Terrorist Threat in America." The ACC's report, combined with aggressive lobbying, had already eroded public right-to-know laws even before the September 11 attack. The willingness of the U.S. Department of Justice to support these rollbacks (but not to reduce chemical hazards) prompted an August 14, 2000, letter to then–attorney general Janet Reno from a number of leading environmental and public interest groups such as the National Environmental Trust and the Sierra Club, along with labor representatives such as the International Chemical Workers Union Council/UFCW, the United Steelworkers of America, and the Paper, Allied-Industrial, Chemical, and Energy Workers International Union. "We are dismayed with the Department's role in impeding community right-to-know about chemical industry dangers while taking no apparent steps to eliminate these hazards at the source," the letter stated.[68]

Many right-to-know rollbacks have focused on the Internet. Shortly after September 11, the Nuclear Regulatory Commission completely shut down its website. The state of Pennsylvania decided to remove environmental information from its site. Risk-management plans, which provide information about the dangers of chemical accidents and how to prevent them, were removed from the website of the U.S. Environmental Protection Agency. The Agency for Toxic Substances and Disease Registry dropped from its website a report on chemical site security, which noted that "security at chemical plants ranged from fair to very poor" and that "security around chemical transportation assets ranged from poor to non-existent."[69]

Of course, there *is* information that should not be published, such as the location of battered women's shelters or the password to your bank account. We are probably better off not publishing recipes for sarin or ricin, but unfortunately that horse has already escaped the barn. According to the Council on Foreign Relations, "Information on how to make such weapons has been available in scientific literature for decades and is now posted on the Internet, and experts say many of the raw materials are not hard to obtain."[70] Likewise, extensive information has already been widely published about bioweapons agents, most of which are naturally occurring.[71]

When it comes to security, in fact, secrecy has a way of backfiring—a point that was noted, ironically enough, in a secret 1977 CIA study that was not declassified until October 2002. "We know that secrecy by its very nature may affect the personality of its practitioners," wrote its author (whose identity still remains a secret). He noted that these "unintended psychological effects . . . seem to diminish rather than enhance security." As an example, he pointed to the attack on Pearl Harbor: "That most disastrous of intelligence failures was due in no small measure to the mishandling of compartmented intelligence. The dissemination of decrypted Japanese communications . . . was so restricted that the theater commanders in Hawaii did not regularly receive them."[72]

The failures of U.S. intelligence information-sharing prior to September 11 provides another possible example of the same phenomenon. Following the attack, members of the House and Senate Intelligence Committees held joint hearings to examine why the FBI and other investigators were unable to detect the terrorist plot before it took place. The investigation revealed that intelligence agencies had many more warnings of possible terrorist attacks than had been previously disclosed to the public. Of course, we can only speculate as to whether greater disclosure might have helped prevent the attack. However, committee staff director Eleanor Hill pointed out that "prior to September 11th, the U.S. intelligence and law enforcement communities were fighting a war against terrorism largely without the benefit of what some would call their most potent weapon in that effort: an alert and committed American public. One need look no further for proof of the latter point than the heroics of the passengers on Flight 93 or the quick action of the flight attendant who identified shoe bomber Richard Reid."[73]

Democracy and the free sharing of information, in other words, may offer our best protection against future terrorist threats. Paradoxically, this is precisely what we may surrender if we allow fear to rule our lives.

6. The Air War

THE NEWS MEDIA offer two basic services to people who are trying to understand the world: information-gathering and information-filtering. For people who are trying to *change* the world, the media provide a third essential service: publicity. These days, the service of information-gathering has been supplanted to a significant degree by the Internet, where it is now possible to instantly access information and opinions about a wide range of topics from a virtually infinite choice of sources. The task of *filtering* all that information, however, has become more important than ever. The broadcast media claim that they deserve the trust of their audiences because their information is produced by professional journalists with expertise and ethical standards that enable them to separate the wheat from the chaff.

In reality, each media outlet filters the news according to a set of priorities and biases that are often not disclosed to its audience. The Fox News Network, for example, purports to offer "fair and balanced" reporting in which "we report, you decide." To see what this means in practice, read the following excerpt from a "fair and balanced" interview conducted by Bill O'Reilly, who calls his program, *The O'Reilly Factor*, a "no-spin zone." On February 24, 2003, O'Reilly interviewed Jeremy Glick, whose father died in the September 11 attacks on the World Trade Center.[1] Unlike O'Reilly, Glick opposed the war in Iraq and had joined with thousands of other Americans in signing a public declaration to that effect. For brevity, we have edited the exchange, but this excerpt will give you the flavor:

O'REILLY: You are mouthing a far left position that is a marginal position in this society, which you're entitled to.

GLICK: It's marginal—*right*.

O'REILLY: You're entitled to it, all right, but you're—you see, even—I'm sure your beliefs are sincere, but what upsets me is I don't think your father would be approving of this.

GLICK: Well, actually, my father thought that Bush's presidency was illegitimate.

O'REILLY: Maybe he did, but—

GLICK: I also didn't think that Bush—

O'REILLY (cuts him off): I don't think he'd be equating this country as a terrorist nation as you are.

GLICK: Well, I wasn't saying that it was necessarily like that.

O'REILLY: Yes, you are. . . . All right. I don't want to—

GLICK: Maybe—

O'REILLY (cuts him off again): I don't want to debate world politics with you.

GLICK: Well, why not? This is about world politics.

O'REILLY: Because, number one, I don't really care what you think. . . .

GLICK: But you do care because you—

O'REILLY (cuts him off again): No, no. Look—

GLICK: The reason why you care is because you evoke 9/11—

O'REILLY (cuts him off again): Here's why I care.

GLICK: —to rationalize—

O'REILLY (interrupts again): Here's why I care—

GLICK: Let me finish. You evoke 9/11 to rationalize everything from domestic plunder to imperialistic aggression worldwide. . . .

O'REILLY: You keep your mouth shut when you sit here exploiting those people. . . . You have a warped view of this world and a warped view of this country.

GLICK: Well, explain that. Let me give you an example of a parallel—

O'REILLY (cuts him off again): No, I'm not going to debate this with you, all right.

GLICK: Well, let me give you an example of parallel experience.
On September 14—

O'REILLY: No, no. Here's—here's the—

GLICK: On September 14—

*O'Reilly cuts him off several more times; Whatever happened
on September 14, Glick never gets the chance to say.*

O'REILLY: Man, I hope your mom isn't watching this.

GLICK: Well, I hope she is.

O'REILLY: I hope your mother is not watching this because
you—that's it. I'm not going to say anymore.

GLICK: OK.

O'REILLY: In respect for your father—

GLICK: On September 14, do you want to know what I'm
doing?

O'REILLY: Shut up! Shut up!

GLICK: Oh, please don't tell me to shut up.

O'REILLY: As respect—as respect—in respect for your father,
who was a Port Authority worker, a fine American, who got
killed unnecessarily by barbarians—

GLICK: By radical extremists who were trained by this government . . .

O'REILLY: Out of respect for him—

GLICK: —not the people of America.

O'REILLY: —I'm not going to—

GLICK: —The people of the ruling class, the small minority.

O'REILLY (to his producer): Cut his mike. I'm not going to dress you down anymore, out of respect for your father. We will be back in a moment with more of THE FACTOR.[2]

Reasoned debates between people with opposing views can provide a useful way of clarifying and understanding the issues that separate them. Viewers who watched this exchange on *The O'Reilly Factor*, however, came away with no better understanding of the respective worldviews of Glick and O'Reilly than they had before watching the show. As O'Reilly stated, he doesn't really *care* what Glick thinks, and he assumes that his viewers don't care either. Why have him as a guest at all, then? Because what the program is really offering is not discussion but *entertainment*—the voyeuristic, sadistic thrill of watching someone get beat up, just like a bullfight or World Wrestling Federation *Smackdown*. O'Reilly's viewers understand this point implicitly. On the day of the broadcast, FreeRepublic.com, a conservative website, received postings from O'Reilly fans who gloated over the exchange with comments including the following:

* "O'Reilly wanted to kick that little punk's ass!"
* "I was waiting for Bill to punch him out. What a piece of crap Glick is."
* "It was very entertaining."
* "Bill should have $itch-slapped that punk-@ss fool."

* "His family will never know how lucky they are that it was O'Reilly only telling him to shut up. Had it been me or my husband, I think America would have been witness to a murder on-air and few juries would have convicted us!"[3]

Of the 219 comments posted to this discussion thread (not counting comments that were deleted because the moderator considered them excessive), 31 advocated subjecting Glick to some form of actual physical violence or humiliation. For O'Reilly and his fans, television is a form of combat—specifically, the "air war." This fact is implicit in O'Reilly's description of his program as a "no-spin zone"—a phrase that parallels and evokes the "no-fly zones" that U.S. jets imposed over Iraqi airspace. As O'Reilly himself has said, a "no-fly zone" and a "no-spin zone" are "the same thing. Violate the rules, get shot down."[4]

The Patriotism Police

Bill O'Reilly's fans at FreeRepublic.com represent the "ground war" that accompanies his air war against "liberal media bias." The ground war—grassroots organizing and pressure—is directed by well-funded organizations such as the Media Research Center (MRC), a conservative "media watchdog." MRC has an annual budget of $7.8 million—roughly ten times the budget of Fairness & Accuracy in Reporting (FAIR), the most prominent media watchdog on the left.[5] MRC sends out daily e-mail alerts to its list of more than 11,000 followers, detailing the alleged bias of media figures such as Dan Rather and Peter Jennings, encouraging the followers to rain complaints onto networks that fail to toe the correct line on Iraq and other issues. In the wake of 9/11, this lobbying took on new intensity. The *New York Times* reported in September 2001 that TV networks were "increasingly coming under criticism from conservatives who say they exhibit a lack of patriotism or are overly negative toward the government." As MSNBC president Erik Sorenson told the *Times*, "Any misstep and you can get into trouble with these guys and have the Patriotism Police hunt you down."[6]

Other attacks on the media have come directly from the Bush administration. After television personality Bill Maher made remarks following 9/11 that were perceived as critical of past U.S. bombing campaigns, White House press secretary Ari Fleischer told journalists that Americans "need to watch what they say, what they do. This is not a time for remarks like this; there never is."[7] In response to complaints about restrictions on civil liberties, Attorney General John Ashcroft testified before Congress, characterizing "our critics" as "those who scare peace-loving people with phantoms of lost liberty; my message is this: Your tactics only aid terrorists—for they erode our national unity and diminish our resolve. They give ammunition to America's enemies, and pause to America's friends. They encourage people of good will to remain silent in the face of evil."[8]

Dennis Pluchinsky, a senior intelligence analyst with the U.S. State Department, went further still in his critique of the

background to Embedding

media. "I accuse the media in the United States of treason," he stated in an opinion article in the *Washington Post* that suggested giving the media "an Osama bin Laden award" and advised, "The president and Congress should pass laws temporarily restricting the media from publishing any security information that can be used by our enemies."[9]

Fox Network owner Rupert Murdoch brilliantly exploited the wartime political environment, in which even extreme nationalistic rhetoric was accepted and popular, while liberals and critics of the White House were pressured to walk softly and carry no stick at all. In addition to Fox, Murdoch owns a worldwide network of 140 sensationalist tabloid newspapers— 40 million papers a week, dominating the newspaper markets in Britain, Australia and New Zealand—all of which adopted editorial positions in support of war with Iraq.[10] In the United States, his *New York Post* called France and Germany an "axis of weasel" for refusing to support Bush's war plans and published a full-page doctored cover photo with the heads of weasels superimposed over the faces of French and German ministers at the United Nations.[11] In France, his paper distributed a story calling French president Jacques Chirac a "worm," illustrated by a large graphic of a worm with Chirac's head.[12]

This sort of imagery has historical precedents. Author Sam Keen, who examined the iconography of war in his 1986 book *Faces of the Enemy*, noted that during wartime, countries frequently produce cartoons, posters and other art that attempt to dehumanize their enemies by "exaggerating each feature until man is metamorphosized into beast, vermin, insect. . . . When your icon of the enemy is complete you will be able to kill without guilt, slaughter without shame."[13] The use of this extreme imagery against erstwhile allies simply for refusing to endorse the U.S. war push represented, in symbolic terms, the Murdoch media's interpretation of the Bush doctrine that "if you are not with us, you are with the terrorists."

At MSNBC, meanwhile, a six-month experiment to develop a liberal program featuring Phil Donahue ended just before the war began, when Donahue's show was cancelled and replaced with a program titled *Countdown: Iraq*. Although the network cited poor ratings as the reason for dumping Donahue, the *New York Times* reported that Donahue "was actually attracting more viewers than any other program on MSNBC, even the channel's signature prime-time program, *Hardball with Chris Matthews*."[14] Further insight into the network's thinking appears in an internal NBC report leaked to AllYourTV.com, a website that covers the television industry. The NBC report recommended axing Donahue because he presented a "difficult public face for NBC in a time of war. . . . He seems to delight in presenting guests who are anti-war, anti-Bush and skeptical of the administration's motives." It went on to outline a possible nightmare scenario where the show becomes "a home for the liberal anti-war agenda at the same time that our competitors are waving the flag at every opportunity."[15] At the same time that Donahue was cancelled, MSNBC added Michael Savage to its lineup, who routinely refers to non-white countries as "turd world nations" and charges that the U.S. "is being taken over by the freaks, the cripples, the perverts and the mental defectives." In one broadcast, Savage justified ethnic slurs as a national security tool: "We need racist stereotypes right now of our enemy in order to encourage our warriors to kill the enemy," he explained—a fairly straightforward summary of Sam Keen's thesis.[16]

The patriotism police also patrolled American radio. Clear Channel Communications owns more than 1,200 radio stations—more than 10 per cent of the U.S. total, and five times more than its closest competitors, CBS and ABC. Its executives have not hesitated to use their power to impose ideological direction. In the weeks leading up to war with Iraq, Clear Channel stations offered financial sponsorship and on-air promotion for pro-war "Rallies for America."[17] A number of Clear Channel stations also pulled the Dixie Chicks from their playlists after the group's lead singer, Natalie Maines, told fans in London that they were ashamed to be from the same state as President Bush. Only a few days previously, Clear Channel Entertainment, the company's concert tour promotional arm, had been enthusiastically promoting its co-sponsorship of 26 concerts in the Chicks' upcoming "Top of the World Tour."[18] In Colorado Springs, two disk jockeys were suspended from Clear Channel affiliate KKCS for defying the ban. Station manager Jerry Grant admitted that KKCS had received 200 calls from listeners, 75 percent of which were from callers who wanted the ban lifted. Nevertheless, he said, he gave the DJs "an alternative:

stop it now and they'll be on suspension, or they can continue playing them and when they come out of the studio they won't have a job."[19] Cumulus Media, another radio conglomerate that owns 262 stations, also banned the Dixie Chicks from all of its country stations.[20] Nationally syndicated radio personality Don Imus told his producer to screen out guests "who come on and whine about how the president failed to explore all diplomatic avenues. Just drop it, because I'm not interested in having that discussion."[21]

Greater diversity could be found in the print media, but prowar voices still predominated. Journalism professor Todd Gitlin tabulated editorials that appeared in the *Washington Post* during a 12-week period shortly before the onset of war and found that "hawkish op-ed pieces numbered 39, dovish ones 12—a ratio of more than 3-to-1."[22]

In addition to restricting the number of anti-war voices on television and radio, media outlets often engaged in selective presentation. The main voices that television viewers saw opposing the war came from a handful of celebrities such as Sean Penn, Martin Sheen, Janeane Garofalo and Susan Sarandon— actors who could be easily dismissed as Brie-eating Hollywood elitists. The newspapers and TV networks could have easily interviewed academics and other more traditional anti-war sources, but they rarely did. In a speech in the Fall of 2002, U.S. senator Edward Kennedy "laid out what was arguably the most comprehensive case yet offered to the public questioning the Bush administration's policy and timing on Iraq," noted ichael Getler, the *Washington Post's* ombudsman. "The next day, the *Post* devoted one sentence to the speech. Ironically, Kennedy made ample use in his remarks of the public testimony in Senate Armed Services Committee hearings a week earlier by retired four-star Army and Marine Corps generals who cautioned about attacking Iraq at this time—hearings that the *Post* also did not cover. Last Saturday, antiwar rallies involving some 200,000 people in London and thousands more in Rome took place and nothing ran in the Sunday *Post* about them. . . . Whatever one thinks about the wisdom of a new war, once it starts it is too late to air arguments that should have been aired before."[23]

Peace groups attempted to purchase commercial time to broadcast ads for peace but were refused air time by all major networks and even MTV. (Some peace groups managed to partially circumvent the ban by buying local time for the ads in major cities.)[24] CBS network president Martin Franks explained the refusal by saying, "we think that informed discussion comes from our news programming." MTV spokesman Graham James said, "We don't accept advocacy advertising because it really opens us up to accepting every point of view on every subject."[25] While pundits from pro-war think tanks generally had ready access to talk shows, it took mass protests of millions of people worldwide on February 15, 2003, before broadcasters gave more than cursory attention to the existence of a large, grassroots peace movement. Even then, coverage consisted of crowd shots and images of people waving banners, with little attempt to present the actual reasoning and arguments put forward by war opponents.

Gulf War II: The Sequel

Media coverage of the 2003 war in Iraq was a sequel, both in style and content, to the 1991 "CNN phenomenon" that occurred during the first U.S. war in the Persian Gulf. "For the first time in history, thanks to the shrewdness of Saddam Hussein, a television network became an active participant in the development of a major international crisis," observed former journalism executive Claude Moisy in a 1995 study titled "The Foreign News Flow in the Information Age." CNN "became the channel of communication between the warring parties and the instant chronicler of the conflict. The impact on the international community was such that the expression 'global live coverage' was widely accepted as the description of what had happened and as the definitive hallmark of CNN."[26]

These trends continued and intensified with media coverage of the 2003 war in Iraq. "By a large margin, TV won in Iraq—even in areas that papers expected to win," reported John Lavine, director of the Readership Institute, a research organization funded by newspapers to help them attract subscribers.[27] The Readership Institute conducted a study of media consumption patterns during the war and found that newspapers were being trounced by TV, which viewers regarded as more complete, accurate and engaging, offering the best experts and the greatest variety of viewpoints.[28]

Within the TV world, moreover, the cable networks domi-nated the traditional nightly news broadcasts on ABC, CBS and NBC. A survey conducted by the *Los Angeles Times* found that nearly 70 percent of Americans were getting most of their infor-mation about the war from the all-news cable channels such as Fox News Network, CNN and MSNBC. Only 18 percent relied on the traditional nightly news.[29] Even MSNBC, whose market share was a distant third behind Fox and CNN, saw a 350 percent increase in viewership during the war.[30] But it was Fox, with its belligerent brand of hyper-patriotism, that won the ratings war.[31] And just as CNN's success in the first war shaped editorial poli-cies throughout the broadcast world, the success of Fox triggered a ripple effect, as other networks tailored their coverage to com-pete with what industry insiders called "the Fox effect."[32]

In many ways, however, the rise of the round-the-clock cable TV news phenomenon reflected a *decline* in the amount and quality of foreign news available to American audiences. As Moisy pointed out, CNN by 1995 had a news-gathering net-work worldwide of only 20 bureaus, with 35 correspondents outside the United States— "only half of what the BBC has had for a long time to cover world events on radio and television" and "only a fraction of what the three largest international newswire services maintain on a permanent basis. . . . The As-sociated Press, a wire service in the United States, . . . can carry up to a hundred foreign stories a day. By comparison, CNN (including CNN International) never brings more than twenty foreign stories a day to its viewers, if for no other reason than the much higher cost of producing and transmitting video news."[33]

With the exception of wars and national disasters, noted *Washington Post* media critic Howard Kurtz, "many news executives, particularly in television, concluded more than a decade ago that Americans had little interest in news beyond their borders." The time devoted to foreign coverage on ABC, CBS and NBC fell from 4,032 minutes in 1989 to 1,382 in 2000, rebounding only slightly following the 9/11 attacks to 2,103 minutes in 2002. Once wars are over, countries fall quickly out of the spotlight. Afghanistan received 306 minutes of coverage while the war raged in November 2001, but within three months it fell to 28 minutes, and by March 2003 it was just one minute. Following the collapse of Saddam's regime, attention to Iraq went into rapid decline, as the cable and TV networks turned to covering the murder of pregnant Californian Laci Peterson and a miracle dog that survived being hit by a car.[34]

Round-the-clock live coverage often comes at the expense of detail, depth and research. It may be visually engaging and emotionally riveting, but viewers receive very little background analysis or historical context. While Operation Desert Storm was underway in 1991, a research team at the University of Massachusetts surveyed public opinion and correlated it with knowledge of basic facts about U.S. policy in the region. The results were startling: "The more TV people watched, the less they knew. . . . Despite months of coverage, most people do not know basic facts about the political situation in the Middle East, or about the recent history of US policy towards Iraq." Moreover, "our study revealed a strong correlation between knowledge and opposition to the war. The more people know, in other words, the less likely they were to support the war policy." Not surprisingly, therefore, "people who generally watch a lot of television were substantially more likely to 'strongly' support the use of force against Iraq."[35]

The same can undoubtedly be said about Gulf War II and the viewers in 2003 who tuned in to watch Fox anchor Neil Cavuto berating a professor who had written an anti-war letter as an "obnoxious, pontificating jerk," a "self-absorbed, condescending imbecile" and an "Ivy League intellectual Lilliputian."[36] Viewers may have *felt* that the coverage on TV was better than the coverage in newspapers, but there was actually an inverse relationship between the amount of emotional entertainment on display and the amount of factual information that viewers received. "Fox does less news and more talking about the news than any other network," noted *Contra Costa Times* TV critic Chuck Barney after reviewing more than 200 hours of war coverage from different channels.[37] However, MSNBC was not far behind. In the excerpt below from an April 2 broadcast (edited here for brevity), note how little information is actually imparted as the program skips over the usual themes: Iraqi joy at being liberated, the evil nature of Saddam and his regime, the dangers of terrorism and weapons of mass destruction, the heroism of our troops, and the iron resolve of President Bush:

ANNOUNCER: And these are the very latest headlines of the top of the hour from MSNBC's continuing coverage of "Operation Iraqi Freedom." . . .

CHRIS MATTHEWS (host): In southern Iraq, residents are still wary of the coalition forces, but they are starting to warm up. Here is ITV's Bill Neely, who is with the British troops in Umm Qasr.

NEELY: Another night, another raid, and another crack is made in the repressive and brutal state that is Saddam's Iraq. The Marines are targeting his henchmen in the south. . . . Saddam's secret police and paramilitaries are being rounded up. The old regime disappears, a new dawn, and some Iraqis are glad to see the last of them. . . .

MATTHEWS: Senator Saxby Chambliss of Georgia sits on the Armed Services Committee, and he is a member of the Senate Select Committee on Intelligence. Senator Chambliss, I'm going to ask you the bottom line: How's the war going?

CHAMBLISS: Chris, I think the war is going great. Our brave men and women are the best trained, best equipped, best prepared army in the world, and in only 13 days, we have moved further with greater speed than any army in the history of the world, and everybody knows what they've seen on TV with respect to the airpower that we're delivering to

Baghdad and other surrounding communities. In Iraq, we're taking out the Republican Guard in a very surgical manner, and at the same time, not destroying civilian sites. We're not destroying a lot of the history of that country, and I think their folks are doing extremely well with a minimum of casualties. . . .

MATTHEWS: Was that the kind of war we should have expected though? A desperate regime, we are facing a desperate regime.

CHAMBLISS: That's right. When you got a guy like Saddam, who is a murderer, a torturer and a rapist, you need to expect all of the worst from him, and now I think we do that, and our guys are prepared for whatever may be forthcoming. . . .

MATTHEWS: Have you got any information about whether they intend to use chemical [weapons]? . . .

CHAMBLISS: I don't know. We know he has them. But whether or not he will use them now, . . . we just don't know, Chris, but it could come in any point in time.

MATTHEWS: Is it fair to assume that the Iraqi government has direct ties to the terrorist camp that's in northern Iraq? . . .

STEVE EMERSON, MSNBC TERRORISM ANALYST: They have found some precursors in some type of chem-bio development there. They're not 100 percent sure; they're shipping it back as we speak for a chemical laboratory analysis. But it looks like—The Commander on site, for example, said there was a precursor to ricin, as it was found in London. . . .

MATTHEWS: Let me ask about the dangers of ricin. How does it affect people? Just give me a basic fear that we should have of that.

EMERSON: It can totally immobilize you, kill you within 36 hours, if not treated within the first few minutes or first hour or so.

MATTHEWS: Once again, great having your expertise. Thanks for joining us. Let's go right now to the White House and NBC's Campbell Brown. How is President Bush handling his role as wartime commander in chief? . . .

BROWN: *USA Today* . . . described the president as carrying a burden, as being very tense, and White House spokesman Ari Fleischer was quick to come out this morning and say he believed the story was too negative, that the president is a lot more steeled, a lot more confident than it made him out to be. . . .

MATTHEWS: Campbell, but the president is in the middle of a war, with Americans getting killed. If he were bopping around the White House singing and whistling dippity doo da, wouldn't people think he was off his nut? Wouldn't you expect him to look a little turned off by what's going on?[38]

As in Gulf War I, the coverage of Gulf War II featured engaging visuals, some of which were familiar, such as the green nightscope shots of Baghdad. Others were new, such as the live videophone images from embedded reporters of troops advancing through the desert. "The characters are the same: The president is a Bush and the other guy is Hussein. But the technology—the military's and the news media's—has exploded," said MSNBC chief Erik Sorenson. He compared it to "the difference between Atari and PlayStation." TV coverage, he said, "will be a much more three-dimensional visual experience, and in some cases you may see war live. This may be one time where the sequel is more compelling than the original."[39]

In Doha, Qatar, the Pentagon built a $1.5 million press center, where Brigadier General Vincent Brooks delivered briefings surrounded by soft-blue plasma screens. Networks quickly scrambled to give names to their war coverage, with corresponding graphic logos that swooshed and gleamed in 3-D colors accompanied by mood-inducing soundtracks. CBS chose "America at War." CNN went with "Strike on Iraq." CNBC used "The Price of War," while NBC and MSNBC both went with "Target: Iraq"—a choice that changed quickly as MSNBC joined Fox in using the Pentagon's own code name for the war—"Operation Iraqi Freedom." The logos featured fluttering American flags or motifs involving red, white and blue. On Fox, martial drumbeats accompanied regularly scheduled updates. Promos for MSNBC featured a photo montage of soldiers accompanied by a piano rendition of "The Star-Spangled Banner." All the networks peppered their broadcasts with statements such as "CNN's live coverage of Operation Iraqi Freedom will continue, right after this short break." Every time this phrase came out of a reporter's mouth or appeared in the corner of the screen, the stations implicitly endorsed White House claims about the motives for war.

The networks also went to pains to identify with and praise the troops. Fox routinely referred to U.S. troops as "we" and "us" and "our folks." MSNBC featured a recurring segment called "America's Bravest," featuring photographs of soldiers in the field. Regular features on Fox included "The Ultimate Sacrifice," featuring images of fallen U.S. soldiers, and "The Heart of War," offering personal profiles of military personnel.

Much of the coverage looked like a prime-time patriotism extravaganza, with inspiring theme music and emotional collages of war photos used liberally at transitions between live reporting and advertising breaks. Bombing raids appeared on the screen as big red fireballs, interspersed with "gun-cam" shots, animated maps, charts and graphics showcasing military maneuvers and weapons technology. Inside the studios, networks provided large, game-board floor maps where ex-generals walked around with pointers, moving around little blue and red jet fighters and tanks.

"Have we made war glamorous?" asked MSNBC anchor Lester Holt during a March 26 exchange with former Navy SEAL and professional wrestler turned politician Jesse Ventura, whom it had hired as an expert commentator.

"It reminds me a lot of the Super Bowl," Ventura replied.[40]

[handwritten margin notes: "Subjectivity / Tabloid element of embeds"]

[handwritten note at bottom: "Glamorization / Sanitization of war"]

Overcoming the "Vietnam Syndrome"

During World Wars I and II, government censorship of military correspondents was routine, heavy and rarely questioned even by the journalists themselves, who engaged in self-censorship and avoided graphic depictions of the gore and emotional trauma of war.[41] This was mostly true also of the Korean War, although censorship was less frequent and journalists began to report on negative aspects of war that previously went unmentioned, such as casualty rates for specific units and morale problems among American soldiers.[42] Vietnam was the first "television war" and also the first war in which serious differences emerged between the military and the reporters who covered it. After the war ended, in fact, many people concluded that television coverage undermined public support for the war by bringing disturbing scenes of death and violence into American living rooms.

This belief is largely a myth, according to University of California, San Diego professor Daniel Hallin, who has extensively studied the content of Vietnam War reporting. "Blood and gore were rarely shown," he states. "The violence in news reports often involved little more than puffs of smoke in the distance, as aircraft bombed the unseen enemy. Only during the 1968 Tet and 1972 Spring offensives, when the war came into urban areas, did its suffering and destruction appear with any regularity on TV. . . . For the first few years of the living room war most

of the coverage was upbeat. . . . In the early years, when morale
was strong, television reflected the upbeat tone of the troops.
But as withdrawals continued and morale declined, the tone of
field reporting changed. This shift was paralleled by developments on the 'home front.' Here, divisions over the war received increasing air time, and the anti-war movement, which
had been vilified as Communist-inspired in the early years, was
more often accepted as a legitimate political movement."[43]

Regardless of whether television coverage *created* anti-war
sentiment or merely *reflected* it, as Hallin suggests, the Vietnam
War marked a watershed in the relationship between the military and the media. In subsequent wars, military planners placed
considerable emphasis on controlling the information that
reached the American public. Journalists were excluded from
the wars in Granada and Panama until the fighting was already
concluded. This in turn led to complaints from journalists, and
in the 1991 war in Iraq, code-named Operation Desert Storm,
the Pentagon adopted a "pool system" through which a hand-
picked group of reporters was allowed to travel with soldiers
under tightly controlled conditions. Between August 1990 and
January 1991 only the "combat pools"—about 23 groups of
reporters—were allowed access to military units in the field. The
Pentagon's Joint Information Bureau, which was responsible for
pool assignments, denied reporters access to some areas of the
war zone on military orders. "For historic purposes, for truth-
telling purposes, there were no independent eyes and ears" to
document all the events of the war, recalled Frank Aukofer, for-

mer bureau chief of the *Milwaukee Journal Sentinel*.[44] As a result, the public saw a largely sanitized version of the war, dominated by Pentagon-supplied video footage of "smart bombs" blowing up buildings and other inanimate targets with pinpoint accuracy. Journalists who refused to participate in the pool system, such as photographer Peter Turnley, captured images of "incredible carnage" but were dismayed that their coverage of the graphic side of war went largely unpublished.[45]

By the time of the 2001 war in Afghanistan, however, reporters had come to identify with the soldiers they were covering. Fox war correspondent Geraldo Rivera went so far as to announce on air that he was carrying a gun (a violation of the rules of war for journalists under the Geneva Convention) and told the *Philadelphia Inquirer* that he hoped to kill Osama bin Laden personally, to "kick his head in, then bring it home and bronze it." Just as reality TV crossed the boundary between journalism and entertainment, Fox and Geraldo crossed the boundary between reporters and combatants. Rather than exclude reporters from the battlefield, the Pentagon realized that it had little to lose and everything to gain by inviting them in. Torie Clarke, the Pentagon's assistant secretary of defense for public affairs, is credited with developing the Pentagon's strategy of "embedding" reporters with troops.[46] Clarke came to the military after running the Washington, D.C., office of the Hill & Knowlton public relations firm, which had run the PR campaign for the government-in-exile of Kuwait during the buildup to Operation Desert Storm a decade earlier. In a 13-page document outlining the ground rules for embedded journalists, the Pentagon stated that "media coverage of any future operation will, to a large extent, shape public perception" in the United States as well as other countries. The system of "embedding" allowed reporters to travel with military units—so long as they followed the rules. Those rules said that reporters could not travel independently, interviews had to be on the record (which meant lower-level service members were less likely to speak candidly), and officers could censor and temporarily delay reports for "operational security."[47] Along with journalists, the Pentagon embedded its own public relations officers, who helped manage the reporters, steering them toward stories and facilitating interviews and photo opportunities.[48]

Overt censorship played a relatively minor role in shaping the content of reports from the field. Far more important was the way embedding encouraged reporters to identify with the soldiers they were covering. Part of the "point of view" to any journalistic account depends on the actual physical location from which reporters witness events. Since much of modern warfare involves the use of air power or long-range artillery, the journalists embedded with troops witnessed weapons being fired but rarely saw what happened at the receiving end. At the same time that hundreds of reporters were traveling with American and British troops, there was almost no journalistic presence in Iraqi cities. Prior to the launch of war, Defense

Department officials warned reporters to clear out of Baghdad, saying that the war would be far more intense than the 1991 war. "If your template is Desert Storm, you've got to imagine something much, much different," said General Richard Myers, chairman of the Joint Chiefs of Staff.[49] Although some print journalists remained in Baghdad, almost all of the television networks took the Pentagon's advice and pulled out in the days immediately preceding the start of fighting.[50] Of the major networks, only CNN still had correspondents in the city on the day the war began.[51] In the absence of their own news teams, the other networks were forced to rely on feeds from CNN and Al Jazeera, the Arabic satellite network once derided by Bush administration officials as "All Osama All the Time."[52]

Embedding also encouraged emotional bonding between reporters and soldiers. CBS News reporter Jim Axelrod, traveling with the Third Infantry, told viewers that he had just come from a military intelligence briefing. "We've been given orders," he said before correcting himself to say, "soldiers have been given orders."[53]

NBC News correspondent David Bloom (who died tragically of a blood clot during the war) said that the soldiers "have done anything and everything that we could ask of them, and we in turn are trying to return the favor by doing anything and everything that they can ask of us."[54]

"They're my protectors," said ABC's John Donovan.[55]

Oliver North, the former marine lieutenant colonel and Iran-Contra defendant turned talk show host, became an embedded reporter for Fox, further blurring the line between journalists and warfighters. "I say General Franks should be commended—that's a U.S. Marine saying that about an Army general," he said in one broadcast.[56]

"Sheer genius," commented U.S. public relations consultant Katie Delahaye Paine, saying that the embedded reporters "have been spectacular, bringing war into our living rooms like never before. . . . The sagacity of the tactic is that it is based on the basic tenet of public relations: it's all about relationships. The better the relationship any of us has with a journalist, the better the chance of that journalist picking up and reporting our messages. So now we have journalists making dozens—if not hundreds—of new friends among the armed forces."[57]

[handwritten: — Objectivity? official approach to embedding]

You're on Combat Camera

In addition to embedded journalists, the Pentagon offered combatants-as-journalists, with its own film crew, called "Combat Camera." In fact, one of the biggest media scoops of the war—the dramatic rescue of POW Jessica Lynch—was a Combat Camera exclusive. *Baltimore Sun* correspondent Ariel Sabar watched the Combat Camera team at work: "A dozen employees at computer stations sift through the 600 to 800 photographs and 25 to 50 video clips beamed in each day from the front lines. About 80% are made available to the news media and the public," he reported. "The images glisten from big screens at the news briefings in the Pentagon and the U.S. Central Command in Qatar. A gallery on the Defense Department Web site gets 750,000 hits a day, triple the number before the war. And for the first time, Combat Camera is e-mailing a daily batch of photographs to major news organizations. . . . In the battlefield of public opinion, experts say, images are as potent as bullets. . . . Photos of sleek fighter jets, rescued POWs, and smiling Iraqis cheering the arrival of U.S. troops are easy to find among Combat Camera's public images. Photos of bombed-out Baghdad neighborhoods and so-called 'collateral damage' are not."[58]

"We've got a lot of good humanitarian images, showing us helping the Iraqi people and the people in Baghdad celebrating," said Lieutenant Jane Laroque, the officer in charge of Combat Camera's soldiers in Iraq. "A lot of our imagery will have a big impact on world opinion."[59]

Outside the United States, however, the imagery that people were seeing was quite different. Instead of heroic soldiers giving candy to Iraqi children and heartwarming rescues of injured POWs, the television networks in Europe and the Arab world showed images of war that were violent, disturbing and unlikely to have the impact that Laroque imagined.

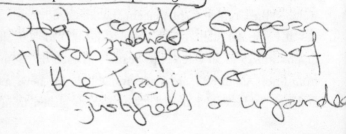

7. As Others See Us

"**LET'S GO TO** CNN's Frank Buckley, who's awaiting the president's dramatic arrival," said CNN's Wolf Blitzer on May 1, 2003. "Tell us, Frank: How dramatic will it be?"

"It will be very dramatic, Wolf," Buckley replied.

Like all good television, the war in Iraq had a dramatic final act, broadcast during prime time—the sunlight gleaming over the waves as the president's fighter jet, with his name and the words "Commander in Chief" painted below the pilot's window, descended from the sky onto the USS *Abraham Lincoln*. The plane zoomed in, snagged a cable stretched across the flight deck and screeched to a stop, and Bush bounded out, dressed in a snug-fitting olive-green flight suit with his helmet tucked under his arm. He strode across the flight deck, posing for pictures and shaking hands with the crew of the carrier. He had even helped fly the jet, he told reporters. "Yes, I flew it," he said. "Yeah, of course, I liked it." Surrounded by gleaming military hardware and hundreds of cheering sailors in uniform, and with the words "Mission Accomplished" emblazoned on a huge banner at his back, he delivered a stirring speech in the glow of sunset that declared a "turning of the tide" in the war against terrorism. "We have fought for the cause of liberty, and for the peace of the world," Bush said. "Because of you, the tyrant has fallen, and Iraq is free."[1]

After the day's festivities, the Democrats got their chance to complain, calling Bush's *Top Gun* act a "tax-subsidized commercial" for his upcoming re-election campaign.[2] They estimated that it had cost $1 million to orchestrate all of the details that made the picture look so perfect.[3] Although White House officials originally claimed that the navy jet was necessary, they later admitted that the aircraft carrier was close enough to shore that a helicopter would have worked just fine. It was so close to shore, in fact, that the aircraft carrier had to be repositioned in the water to keep the TV cameras from picking up the San Diego shoreline.[4] In order to get the light just right and keep the ship from arriving at port before the prime-time broadcast, a Pentagon official admitted, the USS *Abraham Lincoln* made "lazy circles" 30 miles at sea and took 20 hours to cross a distance that could have been covered in an hour or so.[5] Commanders gauged the wind and glided along at precisely that speed so sea breezes would not blow across the ship and create unwanted noise during Bush's speech. When the wind shifted during the speech, the ship changed course.[6]

In the end, though, the spin doctors agreed that the images would stay in the minds of the American people. "It was a pretty darn good photo-op," commented Mike McCurry, President Clinton's former public relations adviser.[7]

"This one is right up there at the top," said Michael Deaver, the former PR man for Ronald Reagan. "It's a great image. It shows American strength, victory. It shows a young president with the courage to do something like this."[8]

"This was not just a speech but a patriotic spectacular, with the ship and its crew serving as crucial backdrops for Bush's remarks, something to cheer the viewing nation and to make Bush look dramatically commander-in-chiefly," wrote *Washington Post* TV critic Tom Shales. "There were several eloquent turns of phrase in the address . . . but they were overwhelmed by the visual impact, pictures both vast and intimate. . . . Everything seemed to go gorgeously right for Bush. Even the pre-sunset lighting was perfect."[9]

Brain Salad Surgery

"You have shown the world the skill and might of the American armed forces," Bush declared during his speech aboard the carrier. "Today . . . with new tactics and precision weapons, we can achieve military objectives without directing violence against civilians. No device of man can remove the tragedy from war. Yet it is a great advance when the guilty have far more to fear from war than the innocent."[10]

As comforting as these words may have seemed to people in the United States, however, the Bush speech sent a different message internationally. Ever since the first U.S.-led war in the Persian Gulf, the United States has won victories with over-whelming displays of military force. From the perspective of many people outside the United States, this is precisely the problem, and the military hardware with which Bush sur-rounded himself struck them as something to fear, not cheer.

The rest of the world did not experience the war as the clean, surgical operation that was presented on U.S. television, where major media outlets cited reasons such as taste, news judgment or concern about offending viewers to explain why they rarely showed images of dead and injured civilians. "It's something we wrestle with every day," said Cecilia Bohand, foreign pictures edi-tor for the *New York Times*. "We're not trying to run posters for the Army, which sometimes it does feel like when we're not running [images of] the other side. Some of us feel we should be a little more graphic." She added that readers reacted with anger on those occasions when the *Times* did push the envelope by pub-lishing a picture of a dead soldier or a dead child. "We're flooded with letters," Bohand said. "Readers don't want to see it."[11]

"It really is disgustingly sanitized on television," said Gene

Bolles, the chief of neurosurgery at Landstuhl, Germany, the destination for the war's most wounded soldiers. Bolles, who operated on Jessica Lynch and other U.S. casualties, said that he had seen "a number of really horrific injuries now from the war. They have lost arms, legs, hands, they have been burned, they have had significant brain injuries and peripheral nerve damage. These are young kids that are going to be, in some regards, changed for life. I don't feel that people realize that."[12]

Writing in the public relations trade press, British-born writer Paul Holmes warned that "we are watching a totally different war from the one seen by the rest of the world," which "has serious long-term implications. It can only deepen the rift between the way the US sees its role in the world and the way the rest of the world sees us. It can also lead to more miscalculations, like the assumption that American invaders would be welcomed as liberators. There may not be much anyone can do at this stage about our image overseas (not that anyone in this administration seems to care), but the US media isn't doing the public any favors by refusing to depict the grim realities of war."[13] *What about UK?*

Questionable given overwhelming conclusions of Cit. review stating otherwise

Cluster Bombs

To get a sense of the difference between U.S. and international patterns in covering the war, we used the LexisNexis database to compile a list of news stories from April 3 through April 10, 2003, that contained the phrases "cluster bombs" and "Iraq."

This period of time was significant because it marked the tail end of the war (the U.S. occupation of Baghdad began on April 9), and also included the first admission by U.S. and British generals that they were using conventional cluster bombs.

Human rights organizations and international relief agencies including Human Rights Watch, Amnesty International, Oxfam International, Christian Aid, and Save the Children have condemned the use of cluster bombs because they kill indiscriminately.[14] Each cluster bomb contains about 200 bomblets the size of a soda can, which disperse upon impact and saturate an area the size of two football fields with explosives and tiny flying shards of steel. Between 5 and 15 percent of the bomblets fail to detonate immediately, leaving behind a deadly litter of unexploded bombs that can continue killing people who happen to encounter them after the battle has ended. "Cluster bombs have a very bad reputation, which they deserve," says Colin King, author of *Jane's Explosive Ordnance Disposal* guide and a British Army bomb-disposal expert from the 1991 Persian Gulf War.[15] Regarded as anti-personnel weapons in the same class as land mines, they have been banned by more than 100 nations in a treaty that the United States has refused to sign. Their use remains legal, therefore, but highly controversial.

During the eight-day period we examined, U.S. publications mentioned cluster bombs only 120 times, even though they accounted for 2,044 of the publications archived in the Lexis-Nexis database. By comparison, Australian and European publications carried 394 stories, while accounting for 673 of the publications listed. In simple ratio terms, this means that European and Australian publications were ten times as likely to mention cluster bombs as their American counterparts.

Numbers alone, however, do not tell the full story. Most of the stories that appeared in U.S. publications mentioned cluster bombs only in passing, characterizing reports of their use as the Iraqi "government line"[16] or making cursory, one-sentence mentions, as in a *New York Times* report on April 8 that said American officials "are investigating reports that cluster bombs were used against villages."[17] Several mentions consisted of denials that cluster bombs were being used, references to their use in *other* wars, or criticisms of their use by Saddam Hussein in past attacks on Kurds and Shiites.

Asked about reports of civilian deaths from cluster bombs in the Hilla region, south of Baghdad, U.S. brigadier general Vincent Brooks responded, "I don't have any specifics about that particular attack and the explosions that would link it to cluster munitions at all."[18] His comments were quickly contradicted by the International Committee of the Red Cross (ICRC), which sent a four-person team to Hilla and found what an ICRC spokesman called a "horror" littered with "dozens of smashed corpses."[19] Amnesty International also investigated and reported as follows:

The scenes at al-Hilla's hospital on 1 April showed that something terrible had happened. The bodies of the men, women and children — both dead and alive — brought to the hospital were punctured with shards of shrapnel from cluster bombs. Videotape of the victims was judged by *Reuters* and *Associated Press* editors as being too awful to show on television. *Independent* [UK] newspaper journalists reported that the pictures showed babies cut in half and children with their limbs blown off. Two lorry-loads of bodies, including women in flowered dresses, were seen outside the hospital.

Injured survivors told reporters how the explosives fell "like grapes" from the sky, and how bomblets bounced through the windows and doors of their homes before exploding. A doctor at al-Hilla's hospital said that almost all the patients were victims of cluster bombs.[20]

Even after admitting that cluster bombs were being used, military spokesmen declined throughout the war to say *how many* were used, saying merely that "an unspecified number of cluster bombs have been fired on Iraq."[21] Other mentions in the U.S. press consisted of statements that talked only about efforts to protect U.S. soldiers from cluster bombs, without mentioning who was dropping them. Several stories, for example, focused on a soldier who suffered a foot injury after stepping on an unexploded bomblet. A *San Francisco Chronicle* report praised soldiers' Kevlar jackets, which help protect them against shrapnel injuries from grenades and cluster bombs.[22]

After the fighting ended, some U.S. media outlets began to report on aspects of the war that they had avoided while the fighting was actually occurring. On April 28, the *Chicago Tri-*

Deembedded post-conflict star
- Restrospective criticism of wa

bune published a picture of the burial of six-year-old Lamiya Ali, an Iraqi girl who was killed along with her eight-year-old sister when she mistook a bomblet for a toy. Several readers, noted *Tribune* editor Don Wycliff, called to complain about the photos, calling them "graphic" and "extremely disturbing" and saying that they showed "no respect for taste or morals, or that poor child's life." In response, Wycliff pointed out that during the entire war, the *Tribune*'s front page had shown "fewer than six" pictures of "dead or grievously wounded bodies."[23]

Air Force General Richard B. Myers, chairman of the Joint Chiefs of Staff, told reporters on April 25 that 1,500 cluster bombs had been used during the war but that only 26 had fallen in civilian areas and that there was only one case of death or injury to a noncombatant. However, Myers's statistic referred only to cluster bombs dropped from airplanes and did not include weapons fired from land-based artillery.[24] In the town of Karbala alone, local civil defense workers who were engaged in post-war cleanup reported harvesting about 1,000 unexploded cluster bombs a day in places that the U.S. said were not targets.[25] "His remarks came amid persistent reports from Baghdad that children and other civilians are being killed or maimed by bomblets that did not explode when they hit their initial targets," reported *Los Angeles Times* writer Greg Miller. "Myers' assertions were challenged by human rights organizations, which said they had learned Friday of new injuries to civilians in Baghdad and other Iraqi cities. . . . Human Rights Watch and other organizations, as well as doctors in Baghdad,

> reported hundreds of casualties from cluster bombs or
> similar devices."[26]

The Arab View

Just as hyper-patriotism has become a successful marketing strategy for the American media, an equal and opposite phenomenon has been occurring in the Muslim and Arab world, where *anti*-Americanism has become the best formula to win ratings. When Arab reporters talked about "weapons of mass destruction" during the Iraq war, they were sometimes referring to cluster bombs.[27] "Arab TV, the networks most prominently led by Al-Jazeera but also including Abu Dhabi TV and others, has clearly emerged as a geopolitical force," noted former FCC chairman Reed Hunt. "This TV, principally by and for Arab audiences, has seen the war through different lenses from those covering the American audience's war. Arab TV has naturally reached an audience willing to accept a view of the war from the defenders' side just as American TV has been broadcast to an audience prone to an opposing view. The natural tendencies of the different audiences, though, have not been challenged by their respective TV mediums but apparently have been exacerbated."[28]

"To fully understand this war and its consequences, it's necessary to watch both Arab and American television," said Rami G. Khouri, a political scientist and editor of the *Daily Star* in

Beirut, Lebanon. Khouri spent the war scanning daily through 20 different Arab and American TV services and found it a "painful exercise, because the business of reporting and interpreting the serious news of war has been transformed into a mishmash of emotional cheerleading, expressions of primordial tribal and national identities, overt ideological manipulation by governments and crass commercial pandering to the masses in pursuit of audience share and advertising dollars." The pattern, he said, was similar on both sides of the ideological divide: "Arab television channels display virtually identical biases and omissions, including: heavy replaying of film of the worst Iraqi civilian casualties; interviews with guests who tend to be critical of the United States; hosts and anchors who jump to debate rather than interview American guests; [and] taking Iraqi and other Arab government statements at face value with little probing into their accuracy."[29]

During the war, Al Jazeera reported a tripling of traffic to its Arab-language website. Its willingness to broadcast images that American networks chose not to display contributed to its popularity. The Google and Lycos search engines reported that "Al Jazeera" had become the most common search term entered by web surfers, with three times more searches than "sex."[30] Simultaneously, Al Jazeera became a target of hacker attacks that kept its English-language site unavailable throughout most of the war and knocked down its Arabic-language site for nearly a week. "No one has ever sustained a crippling attack against a website for so long," noted *USA Today*.[31]

The LexisNexis database contained only a handful of examples of Arab media coverage of the war, but we can get a sense of what Arabs were watching on a daily basis from the following description by British journalist Robert Fisk of video footage shot by the Al Jazeera cable network:

> A remarkable part of the Al-Jazeera tape shows fireballs blooming over western Basra and the explosion of incoming—and presumably British—shells. The short sequence of the dead British soldiers for the public showing, of which Prime Minister Tony Blair expressed such horror, is little different from dozens of similar clips of dead Iraqi soldiers shown on British TV over the past 12 years, pictures that never drew any expressions of condemnation from Blair. . . .
>
> Far more terrible than the pictures of the dead British soldiers, however, is the tape from Basra's largest hospital as victims of the Anglo American bombardment are brought to the operating rooms shrieking in pain. A middle-aged man is carried into the hospital in pajamas, soaked head to foot in blood. A little girl of perhaps 4 is brought into the operating room on a trolley, staring at a heap of her own intestines protruding from the left side of her stomach. A blue-uniformed doctor pours water over the little girl's guts and then gently applies a bandage before beginning surgery. . . .
>
> Other harrowing scenes show the partially decapitated body of a little girl, her red scarf still wound round her neck. Another small girl was lying on a stretcher with her brain

and left ear missing. Another dead child had its feet blown away. There was no indication whether U.S. or British ordnance had killed these children. The tapes give no indication of Iraqi military casualties.[32]

In the American press, Al Jazeera's emphasis was frequently dismissed as evidence of its ideological bias. But bias is itself a highly subjective term. Arab journalists would tell you the same thing that American journalists say in response to similar complaints—that they are simply giving their viewers the coverage they want, and that it is the *American* media that is biased and politically sanitized. The images that most Americans will remember from the war will likely be the toppling of Saddam Hussein's statue, the rescue of American POWs, and soldiers' joyful homecoming reunions with their families. In the Arab world, the images that will come to mind will include the Iraqi boy who lost both of his arms and most of his family in a bombing raid, the Baghdad skyline lit up by bombing, humiliated Iraqi prisoners of war, and angry anti-American protests in the streets.

In Saudi Arabia, *Los Angeles Times* writer Kim Murphy witnessed the effect of those images when she visited the conservative city of Buraydah on April 5. There, she said, "the war in Iraq is gaining new converts every day. . . . If hundreds of young men here haven't left for Baghdad to fight the Americans, it is only because they haven't the means to get there. . . . As television images of the war settle over an increasingly uneasy Arab public, the growing sense of anger and frustration is felt espe-

media war aggravating military war

cially keenly." At mosques throughout the town, she reported, "the noonday air was screeching with dozens of sermons" from clergy like Sheik Suleiman Alwan.

"America and their allies, hell is their destination for the crimes they have committed," Alwan said.

Suleiman Alwan's name is worth noticing. He was one of the sheiks mentioned in December 2001 on the video footage captured in Afghanistan by U.S. soldiers in which Osama bin Laden and several supporters celebrated the 9/11 attacks. An unidentified Saudi sheik who appeared in the video told bin Laden, "Everybody praises what you did," and he mentioned Alwan by name as someone who had given a sermon saying that "this was jihad and those people [killed in the terrorist attack] were not innocent."[33] In fact, one of the 9/11 hijackers, Abdulaziz Alomari, is believed to have been a personal disciple of Alwan and was considered one of his brightest students.

If we have indeed "turned the tide" in the war on terror, as President Bush declared in his speech aboard the aircraft carrier, we should expect that preachers of hatred like Suleiman Alwan are no longer recruiting new converts to serve as foot soldiers and martyrs. The fact that they still are suggests that promises of victory are premature. But it is important also to realize that voices like his are not the only voices speaking in the Muslim world.

Consider, for example, the advice of Prince Moulay Hicham Ben Abdallah of Morocco. "I am a friend of America," he says. "I have flourished in many ways by contact with this fine nation, and I have come to know and respect its people and its founding values."[34] In fact, he was educated and lives in the United States. Known in Morocco as a reformer, he has not hesitated to criticize his own royal family in his advocacy for democracy and human rights in the Muslim world.

"The vast majority of Muslims do not share the tactical or strategic vision, or the interpretation of Islam promoted by these new currents of *jihad* fundamentalism," Hicham said in a September 2002 talk at Princeton University. "Most Muslims want to live in peace and dignity alongside their neighbors of all faiths." He added, however:

We have to acknowledge that bin Laden and his actions have captured the imagination, and even the sympathy, of what is called "the street" in the Arab and Muslim world. This is partly because bin Laden himself projects a fascinating presence on screen and in Arabic, and seems a master of the media event. . . . We must acknowledge, too, that . . . the many democratic movements and progressive civil society organizations that work bravely throughout the Arab and Muslim world have not been as effective in elaborating a consistent discourse that speaks to mass concerns. . . .

Unfortunately, . . . it is hard to avoid the perception that the US is using the "war on terror" as an opportunity to embark on a kind of neo-imperialist project, and that some in the US would not be unhappy to engage in a "clash of civilizations" with the violent *jihadists*, as well as with anyone in

slim world who is not sufficiently submissive to their
in the Muslim world, this only seems to corroborate the
ion of the global *jihadists*, strengthening their appeal at
the expense of more moderate—including moderate fundamentalist—voices.

Perhaps some American strategists now think it will be
easy to roll over these "stirred-up" Muslims with military
force alone. But without a sophisticated concurrent political, diplomatic and especially ideological strategy—one that
distinguishes and isolates the new *jihad* movement from the
Muslim world in general—any military offensive will only
exacerbate the polarization between America and the Islamic world. It will lead to upheavals throughout the Muslim world, in which democratic constituencies will find it
even more difficult to mobilize, and will increase the proba-
bility of prolonged bloody conflicts—whether on the scale of
retail terrorism or of wars between states.[35]

It is impossible, of course, for anyone to predict whether the
Bush administration's bold gamble in Iraq has succeeded or
whether, as Egyptian president Hosni Mubarak warned at the
peak of the war, "there will be 100 bin Ladens afterward."[36] But
in the wake of this conflict, we should ask ourselves whether we
have made the mistake of believing our own propaganda, and
whether we have been fighting the war on terror against the
wrong enemies, in the wrong places, with the wrong weapons.

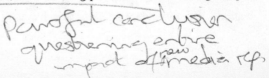

Notes

Unless otherwise indicated, all Internet URLs listed below were visited between the dates of March 31 and May 28, 2003.

Introduction: Liberation Day
1. Matthew Gilbert and Suzanne C. Ryan, "Snap Judgments," *Boston Globe*, April 10, 2003, <http://www.boston.com/news/packages/iraq/globe_stories/041003_snap_judgements.htm>.
2. Ibid.
3. "Pentagon Gets PR Bulls-Eye," *O'Dwyer's PR Daily*, April 11, 2003, <http://www.odwyerpr.com/members/0411pentagon.htm>.
4. "War in Iraq: Photo Gallery," *Boston Globe*, April 9, 2003, <http://www.boston.com/news/packages/iraq/galleries/statue/01a.htm>.

Notes

5. "In Pictures: Saddam Toppled," BBC News, April 9 and 18, 2003, <http://
   news.bbc.co.uk/1/hi/in_depth/photo_gallery/2933629.stm> and <http://
   news.bbc.co.uk/1/hi/in_depth/photo_gallery/2959955.stm>.
6. John Daniszewski, "War with Iraq: A Day to Remember," *Los Angeles
   Times*, April 10, 2003.
7. John W. Rendon, presentation to the Olin Foundation, Information and
   National Security Conference, United States Air Force Academy, Colorado
   Springs, Colo., February 29, 1996, <http://www.rendon.com/docs/airforce.
   html>, (December 19, 1996); available on Internet Archive, <http://web.
   archive.org/web/19970103193930/www.rendon.com/docs/airforce.html>.
8. Ibid.
9. "Air Force Intelligence and Security Doctrine: Psychological Operations
   (PSYOP)," Air Force Instruction 10-702, Secretary of the Air Force, July 19,
   1994, <http://www.fas.org/irp/doddir/usaf/10-702.htm>.
10. "America's Image Further Erodes, Europeans Want Weaker Ties," Pew Re-
    search Center for the People and the Press, March 18, 2003, <http://
    people-press.org/reports/display.php3?ReportID=175>.
11. Anwar Iqbal, "Pro-US Shiite Cleric 'Assassinated,'" United Press Interna-
    tional, <http://www.upi.com/view.cfm?StoryID=20030410-110013-5707r>.
12. "At Least 10 Dead as US Troops in Firefight in Northern Iraq," Agence
    France Presse, April 15, 2003, <http://www.afp.com/english/newsml/
    stories/030415154828.ljmby3zd.html>. See also Jefferson Morley, "Nasiriyah
    Conference Greeted with Suspicion, Satisfaction," *Washington Post*, April 16,
    2003, <http://www.washingtonpost.com/wp-dyn/articles/A37446-2003Apr16.
    html>.
13. Tony Karon, "Wanted: Iraqis to Run Iraq," *Time*, April 15, 2003, <http://
    www.time.com/time/world/printout/0,8816,443918,00.html>.
14. Christopher Dickey and Mark Hosenball, "Banker, Schmoozer, Spy," *News-
    week*, May 12, 2003, <http://www.msnbc.com/news/909076.asp?0cv=KB10>.

1: Branding America

1. George W. Bush, press conference (transcript), Federal News Service, October 11, 2001.
2. "The Role of Public Diplomacy in Support of the Anti-terrorism Campaign," hearing before the Committee on International Relations, U.S.

House of Representatives, 107th Congress, First Session, October 10, 2001, Serial No. 107-47, U.S. Government Printing Office, <http://www.house.gov/international_relations/107/75634.pdf>.

3. Ibid.

4. A number of laws have been passed, beginning with the Gillett Amendment to the Interstate Commerce Commission statute in 1913, which prohibit the use of government funds for the purpose of "publicity" or "public relations." In practice, this has not stopped government agencies from engaging in PR, but other terms are preferred, such as "public information," "public affairs," or "community relations." A study in the mid-1980s by the federal Office of Management and Budget found more than 5,000 people designated as federal information specialists, with an estimated five to seven times that number working in "public affairs" positions. See Michael Turney, "Government Public Relations," <http://www.nku.edu/~turney/prclass/govt.htm>.

5. Henry Hyde and James Sasser, "Speaking to our Silent Allies: the Role of Public Diplomacy in U.S. Foreign Policy" (transcript), Council on Foreign Relations, June 17, 2002, <http://www.cfr.org/publication.php?id=4627>. *Freedom Promotion Act of 2002* (HR 3969), House International Relations Committee, <http://www.house.gov/international_relations/107/freedom.htm>.

6. "War on Terror Is 'Greatest PR Challenge of Generation,'" *Holmes Report*, November 19, 2001, <http://www.holmesreport.com/holmestemp/story.cfm?edit_id=1565&typeid=2>.

7. Ibid.

8. Carla Anne Robbins, "Spin Control," *Wall Street Journal*, October 4, 2001, p. A1.

9. Ibid.

10. Peter Carlson, "The U.S.A. Account," *Washington Post*, December 31, 2001, p. C1, <http://www.washingtonpost.com/ac2/wp-dyn/A43213-2001Dec30>.

11. Michael R. Gordon, "A Nation Challenged," *New York Times*, November 6, 2001, p. A1.

12. Ira Teinowitz, "U.S. Considers Advertising on Al Jazeera TV," *Advertising Age*, October 5, 2001, <http://www.adage.com/news.cms?newsId=33163>.

13. Rance Crain, "Charlotte Beers and the Selling of America," *Advertising Age*, November 5, 2001, <http://www.adage.com/news.cms?newsId=33340>.

Notes

14. "Winning Hearts and Minds," PBS, November 1, 2001, <http://www.pbs. org/newshour/bb/media/july-dec01/heartsminds_11-1a.html>.

15. Ralph Dannheisser, "Beers, Legislators Say Public Diplomacy Vital in Fight on Terror," U.S. Department of State, October 10, 2001, <http://usinfo. state.gov/topical/pol/terror/01101014.htm>.

16. Amol Sharma, "U.S. Hones in on Propaganda War," *Earth Times*, October 13, 2001, <http://www.earthtimes.org/oct/mediaushomesinonoct13_01.htm> June 2, 2002.

17. Joyce Battle, ed., "U.S. Propaganda in the Middle East—the Early Cold War Version," National Security Archive Electronic Briefing Book No. 78, December 13, 2002, <http://www.gwu.edu/~nsarchiv/NSAEBB/NSAEBB78/ essay.htm>.

18. Department of State telegram from Tehran to U.S. Secretary of State, May 2, 1952, <http://www.gwu.edu/~nsarchiv/NSAEBB/NSAEBB78/propaganda% 20061.pdf>.

19. "Notes on Expanded Program for Iran," memorandum from American Embassy, Tehran, to U.S. Department of State, January 12, 1951, <http:// www.gwu.edu/~nsarchiv/NSAEBB/NSAEBB78/propaganda%20016.pdf>.

20. "Motion Pictures: The Film TWO CITIES," memorandum from American Embassy, Tehran, to U.S. Department of State, January 18, 1950, <http://www. gwu.edu/~nsarchiv/NSAEBB/NSAEBB78/propaganda%20004.pdf>.

21. "Collective Security—Your Defense" (script), included in Foreign Service Despatch from American Embassy, Baghdad, to U.S. Department of State, May 16, 1952, <http://www.gwu.edu/~nsarchiv/NSAEBB/NSAEBB78/ propaganda%20062.pdf>.

22. "Anti-Communist Poster Material Prepared by USIS Baghdad," memorandum from American Embassy, Baghdad, to U.S. Department of State, March 10, 1951, <http://www.gwu.edu/~nsarchiv/NSAEBB/NSAEBB78/ propaganda%20021.pdf>.

23. "Proposed Pamphlet Program," from American Embassy, Jidda, to U.S. Department of State, January 8, 1952, <http://www.gwu.edu/~nsarchiv/ NSAEBB/NSAEBB78/propaganda%20046.pdf>.

24. Telegraph from U.S. Embassy, Jidda, to U.S. Secretary of State, September 7, 1952, <http://www.gwu.edu/~nsarchiv/NSAEBB/NSAEBB78/propaganda% 20072.pdf>.

25. "Samples of Anti-Communist Propaganda," Foreign Service Despatch from American Embassy, Baghdad, to Joint State/USIA, March 16, 1954, <http://www.gwu.edu/~nsarchiv/NSAEBB/NSAEBB78/propaganda%20120.pdf>.

26. "Anti-Communist Campaign of Iraq Government," Foreign Service Despatch from American Embassy, Baghdad, to Joint State/USIA, January 13, 1954, <http://www.gwu.edu/~nsarchiv/NSAEBB/NSAEBB78/propaganda%20118.pdf>.

27. John F. Devlin, *The Ba'th Party* (Stanford: Hoover Institution Press, 1976), pp. 108–9, 194; cited in Battle, "U.S. Propaganda in the Middle East—the Early Cold War Version."

28. James Risen, "Secrets of History: The CIA in Iran," *New York Times*, April 16, 2000, <http://www.nytimes.com/library/world/mideast/041600iran-cia-index.html>.

29. Kenneth R. Timmerman, *Fanning the Flames: Guns, Greed & Geopolitics in the Gulf War,* chapter 5, <http://www.iran.org/tib/krt/fanning_ch5.htm>.

30. Martin Ennals, Secretary General of Amnesty International, cited in *Matchbox*, newsletter of Amnesty International USA, Autumn 1976.

31. Michael Dobbs, "U.S. Had Key Role in Iraq Buildup," *Washington Post*, December 30, 2002, p. A1.

32. Joyce Battle, ed., "Shaking Hands with Saddam Hussein: The U.S. Tilts toward Iraq, 1980–1984," National Security Archive Electronic Briefing Book No. 82, February 25, 2003, <http://www.gwu.edu/~nsarchiv/NSAEBB/NSAEBB82/index.htm>.

33. Dobbs, op. cit.

34. Jonathan T. Howe, "Iraq Use of Chemical Weapons," memorandum to the U.S. Secretary of State, November 1, 1983, <http://www.gwu.edu/~nsarchiv/NSAEBB/NSAEBB82/iraq24.pdf>.

35. "Talking Points for Amb. [Ambassador] Rumsfeld's Meeting with Tariq Aziz and Saddam Hussein," United States Interests Section in Iraq Cable from William L. Eagleton, Jr., to the United States Embassy in Jordan, December 14, 1983, <http://www.gwu.edu/~nsarchiv/NSAEBB/NSAEBB82/iraq29.pdf>.

36. "Iraq's Use of Chemical Weapons," press statement by United States Department of State, March 5, 1984, <http://www.gwu.edu/~nsarchiv/NSAEBB/NSAEBB82/iraq43.pdf>.

37. Ibid.

38. Quoted in Seth Ackerman, "The *Washington Post*'s Gas Attack," FAIR/Extra!, September/October 2002, <http://www.fair.org/extra/0209/iraq-gas.html>.

39. Bruce W. Jentleson, *With Friends Like These: Reagan, Bush, and Saddam, 1982–1990* (New York: W. W. Norton, 1994), p. 78.

40. Peter W. Galbraith, "The Wild Card in a Post-Saddam Iraq," *Boston Globe Magazine*, December 15, 2002, <http://www.boston.com/globe/magazine/2002/1215/coverstory.htm>.

41. Douglas Frantz and Murray Waas, "Bush Secret Effort Helped Iraq Build Its War Machine," *Los Angeles Times*, February 23, 1992, p. A1.

42. Philip Shenon, "Iraq Links Germs for Weapons to U.S. and France," *New York Times*, March 16, 2003, <http://www.nytimes.com/2003/03/16/national/16BIO.html>.

43. Transcript for U.S. Senate Armed Services Committee Hearing, September 19, 2002, <http://byrd.senate.gov/byrd_issues/byrd_iraqi_bioweapons/byrd_armedsvc_sept19/byrd_armedsvc_sept19.html>.

44. Secretary Rumsfeld's CNN Interview (transcript), September 21, 2002, <http://www.defenselink.mil/news/Sep2002/t09212002_t921cnn.html>.

45. Detailed notes of Rumsfeld's meeting with Saddam Hussein show no mention of chemical weapons. See "Rumsfeld Mission: December 20 Meeting with Iraqi President Saddam Hussein," telegraph from American Embassy, London, to U.S. Secretary of State, December 21, 1983, <http://www.gwu.edu/~nsarchiv/NSAEBB/NSAEBB82/iraq31.pdf>.

Rumsfeld did mention chemical weapons briefly in a separate meeting with Iraqi Foreign Minister Tariq Aziz, but his comments do not qualify as a warning. To the contrary, Rumsfeld declared that the U.S. and Iraq had "more similarities than differences," expressed a desire to prevent Iraq from losing its war with Iran, and said that "our efforts to assist were inhibited by certain things that made it difficult for us," citing the use of chemical weapons, possible escalation in the gulf, and human rights. See "Rumsfeld One-on-One Meeting with Iraqi Deputy Prime Minister and Foreign Minister Tariq Aziz," telegraph from American Embassy, London, to U.S. Secretary of State, December 21, 1983 <http://www.gwu.edu/~nsarchiv/NSAEBB/NSAEBB82/iraq32.pdf>.

46. Ira Teinowitz, "Charlotte Beers and the Selling of America," *Advertising Age*, September 23, 2002, <http://www.adage.com/news.cms?newsId=36106>.

47. Tony Karon, "The War for Muslim Hearts and Minds," *Time*, November 6, 2001, <http://www-unix.oit.umass.edu/~commdept/resources/gulfwar.html>.

48. Ibid.

49. Margaret Carlson, "Can Charlotte Beers Sell Uncle Sam?" *Time*, November 14, 2001, <http://www.time.com/time/columnist/carlson/article/0,9565,184536,00.html>.

50. Peter Carlson, op. cit.

51. Margaret Carlson, op. cit.; *NewsHour with Jim Lehrer* (transcript), February 18, 2002, <http://www.pbs.org/newshour/bb/media/jan-june02/public_2-18.html>.

52. Charlotte Beers and Richard Boucher at the Foreign Press Center (transcript), November 9, 2001, U.S. Department of State, <http://usinfo.state.gov/usa/islam/t111401.htm>.

53. Anna Kuchment, "Selling the USA," *Newsweek*, November 26, 2001, p. 66.

54. "The Battle for Hearts and Minds," *Economist*, November 9, 2001, <http://www.economist.com/agenda/displayStory.cfm?story_id=861388>.

55. Neil MacFarquhar, "Many Arabs Say Bush Misreads Their History and Goals," *New York Times*, January 31, 2002, <http://www.nytimes.com/2002/01/31/international/middleeast/31ARAB.html>.

56. Ibid.

57. Ibid.

58. Charlotte Beers, "Funding for Public Diplomacy," statement before the Subcommittee on Commerce, Justice, and State of the House Appropriations Committee, Washington, D.C., April 24, 2002, <http://www.state.gov/r/us/9778.htm>.

59. Jane Perlez, "Muslim-As-Apple-Pie Videos Are Greeted with Skepticism," *New York Times*, October 30, 2002, <http://www.nytimes.com/2002/10/30/international/asia/30INDO.html>.

60. Dan Murphy, "U.S. Ads Miss Mark, Muslims Say," *Christian Science Monitor*, January 7, 2003, <http://www.csmonitor.com/2003/0107/p06s01-woap.html>.

61. Lynette Clemetson and Nazila Fathi, "U.S.'s Powerful Weapon in Iran: TV," *New York Times*, December 7, 2002.

62. Felicity Barringer, "U.S. Messages to Arab Youth, Wrapped in Song," *New York Times*, June 17, 2002, <http://www.nytimes.com/2002/06/17/international/middleeast/17RADI.html>.

63. Michael Z. Wise, "U.S. Writers Do Cultural Battle Around the Globe," *New York Times*, December 7, 2002, <http://www.nytimes.com/2002/12/07/arts/07WRIT.html>.

64. Charlotte Beers, "Public Diplomacy After September 11," Remarks to the National Press Club, December 18, 2002, <http://www.state.gov/r/us/16269.htm>.

65. Mark O'Keefe, "State Department Draws Fire in Effort to Promote Muslim Life in U.S.," Newhouse News Service, May 14, 2002, <http://www.newhouse.com/archive/story1b051402.html>.

66. Council of American Muslims for Understanding (website), <http://www.opendialogue.com>.

67. Naomi Klein, "America Is Not a Hamburger," *Guardian* (UK), March 14, 2002, <http://www.guardian.co.uk/Archive/Article/0,4273,4373814,00.html>.

68. Murphy, op. cit.

69. Beers, "Public Diplomacy After September 11."

70. "U.S. Propaganda Pitch Halted," CBS News, January 16, 2003, <http://www.cbsnews.com/stories/2003/01/16/world/main536756.shtml>.

71. Colin L. Powell, "Departure of Charlotte Beers, Under Secretary for Public Diplomacy and Public Affairs" (news release), March 3, 2003, <http://www.state.gov/secretary/rm/2003/18129.htm>.

72. Kevin McCauley, "Saddam, PR Genius," *O'Dwyer's PR Daily*, February 26, 2003, <http://www.odwyerpr.com/members/archived_stories_2003/february/0226saddam.htm>.

73. Carl Weiser, "How to Sell America to People Who Hate It," Gannett News Service, October 14, 2001, <http://www.prfirms.org/resources/news/sell_hate101401.asp>.

74. William Douglas, "Bush Relies on Advertising Experts to Win Over Muslims," *Sydney Morning Herald*, October 25, 2001, <http://old.smh.com.au/news/0110/25/world/world10.html>.

2: War Is Sell

1. Elisabeth Bumiller, "Bush Aides Set Strategy to Sell Policy on Iraq," *New York Times*, September 7, 2002, p. A1.

2. Karen DeYoung, "Bush to Create Formal Office to Shape U.S. Image Abroad," *Washington Post*, July 30, 2002, p. A1, <http://www.washingtonpost.com/ac2/wp-dyn/A18822-2002Jul29>.

3. Tim Reid, "America Plans PR Blitz on Saddam," *Times* (UK), September 17, 2002, <http://www.timesonline.co.uk/article/0,,3-418110,00.html>.

4. Martha Brant, "Ladies and Gentlemen . . . the Band: Selling the War in Iraq," *Newsweek*, September 18, 2002, <http://www.msnbc.com/news/809682.asp>, (September 18, 2002).

5. Douglas Quenqua, "Pentagon Seeks PR Advice Before Diplomatic Attempt," *PR Week*, August 26, 2002, <http://www.prweek.com/news/news_story.cfm?ID=156288&site=3>.

6. Eli J. Lake, "US Pushes PR for War with Iraq," United Press International, August 20, 2002, <http://www.upi.com/view.cfm?StoryID=20020820-050908-1065r>.

7. Douglas Quenqua, "Bush's Calculated Pursuit of Validation Has Its Costs," *PR Week*, September 16, 2002.

8. Ibid.

9. Alison Mitchell and Adam Nagourney, "G.O.P. Gains from War Talk but Does Not Talk About It," *New York Times*, September 21, 2002, <http://www.nytimes.com/2002/09/21/politics/21REPU.html>.

10. Arthur E. Rowse, "Flacking for the Emir," *Progressive*, May 1991, p. 22.

11. "Showdown With Saddam," ABC News, February 7, 1998, <http://more.abcnews.go.com/sections/world/cia/cia.html>.

12. Stephen J. Hedges, "U.S. Pays PR Guru to Make Its Points," *Chicago Tribune*, May 12, 2002.

13. Mark Atkinson, "Propagandist for Hire," and "The CIA's Secret War in Iraq," ABC News, February 7, 1998, <http://more.abcnews.go.com/sections/world/cia/rendon.html> and <http://more.abcnews.go.com/sections/world/cia/plot.htm>.

14. Robert Dreyfuss, "Tinker, Banker, NeoCon, Spy," *American Prospect*, vol. 13, issue 21, November 18, 2002, <http://www.prospect.org/print-friendly/print/V13/21/dreyfuss-r.html>.

15. Ibid.

16. Stephen Fidler and Roula Khalaf, "Ahmad Chalabi Divides Opinion Within the Opposition Movement and Among Those in Washington Planning Regime Change," *Financial Times* (London), December 13, 2002, p. 19.

17. Ibid.

18. Michael Dobbs, "Old Strategy on Iraq Sparks New Debate," *Washington Post*, December 27, 2001, p. A1.

Notes

19. Fidler and Khalaf, op. cit.
20. Robin Wright, "Aid: Support for the Iraqi National Congress Has Waned Amid the Group's Missteps on Funding and Recruiting," *Los Angeles Times*, March 20, 2001.
21. "About PNAC" and Letter to U.S. President William J. Clinton, Project for the New American Century, January 26, 1998, <http://www.newamericancentury. org/aboutpnac.htm> and <http://www.newamericancentury.org/iraqclin tonletter.htm>.
22. Foreign Agents Registration Act (FARA) filing for Iraq, Second Semi-Annual Report for 2000, U.S. Department of Justice, <http://www.usdoj.gov/criminal/ fara/fara2nd00/COUNTRY/IRAQ.HTM>.
23. "US Options in Confronting Iraq," hearing before the Committee on International Relations, House of Representatives, 105th Congress, Second Session, February 25, 1998, <http://commdocs.house.gov/committees/intlrel/ hfa48782.000/hfa48782_0.HTM>.
24. Letter to U.S. President George W. Bush, Project for the New American Century, September 20, 2001, <http://www.newamericancentury.org/Bush letter.htm>.
25. Warren P. Strobel and Jonathan S. Landay, "Pentagon Hires Public Relations Firm to Reverse Opposition in Islamic World," Knight Ridder, October 17, 2001, <http://www.prfirms.org/resources/news/pentagon101901. asp>.
26. James Dao and Eric Schmitt, "Pentagon Readies Efforts to Sway Sentiment Abroad," *New York Times*, February 18, 2002, <http://www.nytimes. com/2002/02/19/international/19PENT.html>.
27. Lou Morano, "Propaganda: Remember the Kuwaiti Babies?" United Press International, February 26, 2002, <http://www.propagandacritic.com/articles/ examples.osi.html>.
28. Colin James, "Moran's Secret Crusade Against the Tyranny of Saddam," *Adelaide Advertiser* (Australia), April 5, 2003, <http://www.theadvertiser. news.com.au/printpage/0,5942,6239116,00.html>.
29. Seymour Hersh, "Annals of National Security: The Debate Within," *New Yorker*, March 11, 2002, <http://www.newyorker.com/fact/content/?020311fa_ FACT>.
30. Ibid.

31. "Who Will Control Iraq's Oil in Future?" *Intelligence Online*, September 27, 2002.

32. Robert Dreyfuss, "The Pentagon Muzzles the CIA," *American Prospect*, vol. 13, issue 22, December 16, 2002, <http://www.prospect.org/print-friendly/print/V13/22/dreyfuss-r.html>.

33. Ibid.

34. "CLI Confirms Iraqi Declaration 'Clearly Non-Compliant'" (news release), U.S. Newswire, December 19, 2002. See also "CLI Affiliations," <http://www.endthewar.org/whoiscli3.htm>; website for the Project for the New American Century, <http://www.newamericancentury.org>; and website for the American Enterprise Institute, <http://www.aei.org>.

35. Mission Statement, Committee for the Liberation of Iraq, <http://www.liberationiraq.org>.

36. "Group Formed to Promote Freedom in Iraq" (news release), Committee for the Liberation of Iraq, <http://www.liberationiraq.org/press_releases/archives/00000001.htm>.

37. Biography of Randy Scheunemann, Project on Transitional Democracies (website), <http://www.projecttransitionaldemocracy.org/html/bios/scheunemann.htm>.

38. Peter Slevin, "New Group Aims to Drum Up Backing for Ouster," *Washington Post*, November 4, 2002, p. A15, <http://www.washingtonpost.com/ac2/wp-dyn/A64233-2002Nov3>.

39. Eric Schmitt, "New Group Will Lobby for Change in Iraqi Rule," *New York Times*, November 15, 2002, <http://www.nytimes.com/2002/11/15/international/middleeast/15HAWK.html>.

40. Douglas Quenqua, "Opinion Leaders Unite to Shift Saddam Focus in US," *PR Week*, November 25, 2002, <http://www.prweek.com/news/news_story.cfm?ID=164666&site=3>.

41. Douglas Quenqua, "US Training Iraqis in Media to Raise Support for Attack," *PR Week*, September 2, 2002, <http://www.prweek.com/news/news_story.cfm?ID=156687&site=3>.

42. Robin Wright, "United States to Train Iraqis in Rhetoric Against Hussein," *Los Angeles Times*, August 25, 2002.

43. Quenqua, "US Training Iraqis in Media to Raise Support for Attack."

44. Muhammed Eshaiker, interview with *On the Media*, National Public Radio, August 30, 2002.

45. "Target: Iraq" (transcript), NBC News, March 21, 2003.

46. On May 21, 2002, Rev. Moon gave a speech at the 20th anniversary of the founding of the *Washington Times*, discussing its role within his "family" of media projects, which now includes United Press International. See "Freedom, Family and Faith: The Role of the Media in the 21st Century," on the Unification Church website at <http://www.unification.net/2002/20020521_1.html>.

47. Lawrence E. Walsh, "Final Report of the Independent Counsel for Iran/Contra Matters," August 4, 1993, <http://www.fas.org/irp/offdocs/walsh/>; see also Michael Ledeen, *Perilous Statecraft: An Insider's Account of the Iran-Contra Affair* (New York: Scribner, 1988).

48. Richard Pipes and Laurie Mylroie, "Back Iraq: It's Time for a U.S. Tilt," *New Republic*, April 27, 1987.

49. Joe Hagan, "She's Richard Perle's Oyster," *New York Observer*, April 7, 2003, <http://www.observer.com/pages/frontpage3.asp>.

50. Brian Whitaker, "US Thinktanks Give Lessons in Foreign Policy," *Guardian* (UK), August 19, 2002, <http://www.guardian.co.uk/elsewhere/journalist/story/0,7792,777100,00.html>.

51. U.S. Committee for a Free Lebanon (website), <http://www.freelebanon.org>; "A Petition Demanding War Against Governments that Sponsor Terrorism," <http://www.petitiononline.com/CAAT/petition.html>.

52. Hagan, op. cit.

53. Thom Shanker, "A Nation at War; Vanguard; Iraqi Fighters, Hussein Foes, Are Flown into the South," *New York Times*, April 7, 2003, p. A7.

54. Ibid.

55. Sudarsan Raghavan, "Iraq's Fresh 'Freedom Fighters' a Mix of West, East, Young, Old," *San Jose Mercury News*, April 17, 2003, <http://www.bayarea.com/mld/mercurynews/news/special_packages/iraq/5653822.htm>.

56. John Kifner and Craig S. Smith, "Iraqis March, Want U.S. Out Pronto," *New York Times*, April 19, 2003, <http://www.nwanews.com/adg/story_National.php?storyid=27629>.

57. David Ignatius, "Bush's Confusion, Baghdad's Mess," *Washington Post*, April 23, 2003, p. A35, <http://www.washingtonpost.com/wp-dyn/articles/A18344-2003Apr22.html>.

58. David Rohde, "Political Party in Mosul Emerges with Own Army," *New York Times*, April 18, 2003, <http://www.nytimes.com/2003/04/18/international/worldspecial/18NORT.html>.

59. Stanley Reed, "In Baghdad, Guns, Chaos . . . Enterprise," *BusinessWeek*, May 2, 2003.

60. Carol Morello, "'Nucleus' of Iraqi Leaders Emerges," *Washington Post*, May 6, 2003, p. A1, <http://www.washingtonpost.com/wp-dyn/articles/A17929-2003 May5.html>.

3: True Lies

1. U.S. Department of Defense news briefing (transcript), September 25, 2001, <http://www.fas.org/sgp/news/2001/09/dod092501.html>.

2. James Dao and Eric Schmitt, "Pentagon Readies Effort to Sway Opinion Abroad," *New York Times*, February 19, 2002, <http://www.nytimes.com/2002/02/19/international/19PENT.html>.

3. Eric Schmitt, "Pentagon May Eliminate New Office of Influence," *New York Times*, February 19, 2002, <http://www.nytimes.com/2002/02/25/politics/25CND-MILI.html>.

4. Secretary Rumsfeld Media Availability En Route to Chile (transcript), November 18, 2002, <http://www.defenselink.mil/news/Nov2002/t11212002_t1118sd2.html>.

5. *Information Operations*, Air Force Doctrine Document 2-5, August 5, 1998, i–ii, viii, 4–5, 11, 13, <http://www.cadre.maxwell.af.mil/warfarestudies/iwac/AFDocs/afdd2-5.pdf>.

6. "Citizens for Free Kuwait Files with FARA After a Nine-month Lag," *O'Dwyer's FARA Report*, Vol. 1, No. 9, October 1991, p. 2.

7. Ibid.

8. Arthur E. Rowse, "Flacking for the Emir," *Progressive*, May 1991, pp. 21–22.

9. *O'Dwyer's PR Services Report*, Vol. 5, No. 1, January 1991, p. 1.

10. John MacArthur, *The Second Front: Censorship and Propaganda in the Gulf War*, (Berkeley, Calif.: University of California Press, 1992), p. 58.

11. Ibid.

12. "Iraq/Occupied Kuwait: Human Rights Violations Since August 2, 1990," Amnesty International, December 19, 1990, p. 66.

13. MacArthur, op. cit., p. 84.

14. "Fitz-Pegado Works for Cayman Islands," *O'Dwyer's PR Daily*, May 28, 2002, <http://www.odwyerpr.com/members/archived_stories_2002/may/0528pegado.htm>. For a more detailed account of Hill & Knowlton's PR work for Kuwait, see John Stauber and Sheldon Rampton, *Toxic Sludge Is Good for You!* (Monroe, Maine: Common Courage Press, 1995), pp. 167–75.

15. *ABC World News Tonight*, March 15, 1991.

16. Robert L. Jackson, "Former U.S. Envoy, Two Others Charged in Gulf War Scheme," *Los Angeles Times*, July 8, 1992, p. A1.

17. Michael Ross, "Doubts Cast on Girl's Account of Iraqi Atrocities in Kuwait," *Los Angeles Times*, January 7, 1992, p. A8.

18. Aziz Abu-Hamad, "Focus on Proven Abuses," letter to the editor, *Washington Post*, April 4, 1993, p. C6.

19. MacArthur, op. cit., pp. 51–53.

20. Joost R. Hiltermann, "America Didn't Seem to Mind Poison Gas," *International Herald Tribune*, January 17, 2003, <http://www.iht.com/articles/83625.html>.

21. "Activism Update: HBO Adds Disclaimer to Gulf War Movie," Fairness and Accuracy in Media, January 3, 2003, <http://www.fair.org/activism/hbo-incubators-update.html>.

22. Tom Shales, "'Live From Baghdad': The Cameras of War," *Washington Post*, December 7, 2002, p. C1, <http://www.washingtonpost.com/ac2/wp-dyn?pagename=article&node=&contentId=A21263-2002Dec6>.

23. "Americans Thinking About Iraq, But Focused on the Economy," Midterm Election Preview, Pew Research Center for the People and the Press, October 10, 2002, <http://people-press.org/reports/display.php3?ReportID=162>.

24. Martin Merzer, "Poll: Majority Oppose Unilateral Action Against Iraq," *Miami Herald*, January 12, 2003, <http://www.miami.com/mld/miamiherald/4911975.htm>.

25. "Genocide in Iraq: The Anfal Campaign Against the Kurds," Human Rights Watch, July 1993, <http://www.hrw.org/reports/1993/iraqanfal/>.

26. "Fact Sheet: Iraq's Nuclear Weapon Programme," International Atomic Energy Agency, December 27, 2002, <http://www.iaea.org/worldatom/Programmes/ActionTeam/nwp2.html>.

27. "Iraq: The UNSCOM Experience," Stockholm International Peace Research Institute, October 1998, <http://editors.sipri.se/pubs/Factsheet/unscom.html>.

28. "Spying on Saddam," interview with Barton Gellman, PBS, April 27, 1999, <http://www.pbs.org/wgbh/pages/frontline/shows/unscom/interviews/gellman.html>.

29. Ibid.

30. John Barry, "The Defector's Secrets," *Newsweek*, March 3, 2003.

31. General Hussein Kamel, transcript of meeting with Prof. M. Zifferero (IAEA) and Nikita Smidovich (UNSCOM) in Amman, Jordan, August 22, 1995, pp. 12–13, <http://www.fair.org/press-releases/kamel.pdf>.

32. Scott Ritter, "Is Iraq a True Threat to the US?" *Boston Globe*, July 20, 2002, <http://www.commondreams.org/views02/0721-02.htm>.

33. Joseph Curl, "Agency Disavows Report on Iraq Arms," *Washington Times*, September 27, 2002, <http://www.washtimes.com/national/20020927-500715.htm>.

34. Ibid.

35. George W. Bush, "President's Remarks at the United Nations General Assembly," September 12, 2002, <http://www.whitehouse.gov/news/releases/2002/09/20020912-1.html>.

36. Joby Warrick, "U.S. Claim on Nuclear Weapon Program Is Called into Question," *Washington Post*, January 24, 2003, <http://www.washingtonpost.com/ac2/wp-dyn?pagename=article&node=&contentId=A35360-2003Jan23>.

37. Dana Milbank, "For Bush, Facts Are Malleable," *Washington Post*, October 22, 2002.

38. "President Bush Outlines Iraqi Threat," remarks by the President on Iraq, Cincinnati Museum Center—Cincinnati Union Terminal, Cincinnati, Ohio, October 7, 2002, <http://www.whitehouse.gov/news/releases/2002/10/20021007-8.html>.

39. Ibid.

40. Kamel interview, p. 5.

41. Luis Charbonneau, "U.N. Official: Fake Iraq Nuke Papers Were Crude," Reuters, March 25, 2003, <http://asia.reuters.com/newsArticle.jhtml?type=topNews&storyID=2444571>.

42. Henry Waxman, letter to President George W. Bush, March 17, 2003, <http://www.fas.org/irp/news/2003/03/waxman.pdf>.

43. *Face the Nation*, CBS News, October 20, 2002, <http://www.cbsnews.com/stories/2002/10/21/ftn/main526319.shtml>.

44. George J. Tenet, letter to Bob Graham, Congressional Record, October 9, 2002, p. S10154, <http://www.fas.org/irp/news/2002/10/dci100702.html>.

45. Dafna Linzer, "Banned Missiles Fired at U.S. Troops," *San Francisco Examiner*, March 21, 2003, <http://examiner.com/headlines/default.jsp?story=n.missiles.0321w>.

46. Paul Richter, "War with Iraq; Military Strategy; Revamped Patriot System Downs 2 Missiles Aimed at US Forces," *Los Angeles Times*, March 21, 2003.

47. Deb Riechmann, "Dark Iraq War Scenarios Haven't Happened," *News-Journal* (Longview, Texas), April 11, 2003, <http://www.news-journal.com/news/content/news/ap_story.html/Intl/AP.V4462.AP-War-Worst-Hasn.html>.

48. David Pugliese, "Scud Missiles Remain Thorn for US Forces," *Windsor Star* (Canada), March 21, 2003, p. A8.

49. "The War in Iraq by the Numbers," *Edmonton Journal*, April 14, 2003, p. A4.

50. Chris Hedges and Donald G. McNeil, Jr., "New Clue Fails to Explain Iraq Role in Sept. 11 Attack," *New York Times*, December 16, 2001, <http://www.nytimes.com/2001/12/16/international/middleeast/16IRAQ.html>.

51. Walter Pincus, "No Link Between Hijacker, Iraq Found, U.S. Says," *Washington Post*, May 1, 2002, p. A9.

52. James Risen, "Prague Discounts an Iraqi Meeting," *New York Times*, October 21, 2002, <http://www.nytimes.com/2002/10/21/international/21PRAG.html>.

53. Wolfowitz Interview with the *San Francisco Chronicle* (transcript), U.S. Department of Defense, February 23, 2002, <http://www.defenselink.mil/news/Feb2002/t02272002_t0223sf.html>.

54. Bob Drogin and Paul Richter, "White House Backs Report of Link between Iraq, Sept. 11 Suspect," *Los Angeles Times*, August 2, 2002, <http://www.kansascity.com/mld/kansascity/news/local/3782550.htm>.

55. Bob Drogin, Paul Richter and Doyle McManus, "White House Says Sept. 11 Skyjacker Had Met Iraqi Agent," *Los Angeles Times*, August 5, 2002.

56. Gary Leupp, "Perle's Bombshell in Milan," *Outlook India*, September 10, 2002, <http://www.outlookindia.com/full.asp?fname=gary&fodname=20020911&sid=1>.

57. *Meet the Press* (transcript), September 8, 2002, <http://www.mtholyoke.edu/acad/intrel/bush/meet.htm>.

58. Andrea Mitchell, "The Iraq and al-Qaida Connection," NBC News, October 31, 2002, <http://www.msnbc.com/news/824024.asp>.

59. "Iraq—Its Infrastructure of Concealment, Deception and Intimidation," Office of British Prime Minister Tony Blair, January 2003, <http://www.number-10.gov.uk/files/pdf/Iraq.pdf>.

60. Colin Powell, "Remarks to the United Nations Security Council," February 5, 2003, <http://www.state.gov/secretary/rm/2003/17300.htm>.

61. Ibrahim al-Marashi, "Iraq's Security and Intelligence Network: A Guide and Analysis," *Middle East Review of International Affairs*, vol. 6, no. 3, September 2002, <http://meria.idc.ac.il/journal/2002/issue3/jv6n3a1.html>.

62. Michael White and Brian Whitaker, "UK War Dossier a Sham, Say Experts," *Guardian* (UK), February 7, 2003, <http://www.guardian.co.uk/Iraq/Story/0,2763,890916,00.html>.

63. Rosemary Bennett and Elaine Monaghan, "Iraq Dossier Assembled by Junior Aides," *Times Online* (UK), February 8, 2003, <http://www.timesonline.co.uk/article/0,,2-570248,00.html>.

64. Gary Gibbon, "No. 10 Admits Dossier Blunder," *Channel 4 News* (UK), February 7, 2003, <http://www.channel4.com/news/2003/02/week_1/07_dossier.html>.

65. Gaby Hinsliff, Martin Bright, Peter Beaumont and Ed Vulliamy, "First Casualties in the Propaganda Firefight," *Observer* (UK), February 9, 2003, <http://www.observer.co.uk/iraq/story/0,12239,892145,00.html>. The material plagiarized from *Jane's Intelligence Review* included Ken Gause, "Can the Iraqi Security Apparatus Save Saddam?" November 2002, pp. 8–13; and Sean Boyne, "Inside Iraq's Security Network," which appeared in two parts in July 1997 and August 1997.

66. Glenn Frankel, "Blair Acknowledges Flaws in Iraq Dossier," *Washington Post*, February 8, 2003, <http://www.washingtonpost.com/ac2/wp-dyn/A42276-2003Feb7>.

67. "Britain's Intelligence Crisis," *Jane's Intelligence Digest*, February 14, 2003, <http://www.janes.com/regional_news/europe/news/jid/jid030214_1_n.shtml>.

68. "Leaked Report Rejects Iraqi Al-Qaeda Link," BBC, February 5, 2003, <http://news.bbc.co.uk/2/hi/uk_news/2727471.stm>. See also Raymond Whitaker, "MI6 and the CIA: The Enemy Within," *New Zealand Herald*,

February 9, 2003, <http://www.nzherald.co.nz/storydisplay.cfm?storyID= 3100174>.

69. Luke Harding, "Revealed: Truth Behind U.S. 'Poison Factory' Claim," *Observer* (UK), February 9, 2003, <http://www.observer.co.uk/iraq/story/0,12239, 892112,00.html>.

70. Joseph Logan, "Islamic Kurds Accuse U.S. of Bombing Them by Mistake," Reuters AlertNet, March 26, 2003, <http://www.alertnet.org/thenews/news desk/LO2647211.htm>.

71. "Patterns of Global Terrorism 2001," United States Department of State, May 2002, p. 65, <http://www.state.gov/documents/organization/10319.pdf>.

72. "Kurdish Rebels to End Armed Struggle," BBC News, August 5, 1999, <http://news.bbc.co.uk/1/hi/world/europe/412577.stm>.

73. Ibid., pp. 51, 59.

74. "Saudi Arabia: End Secrecy and Suffering," Amnesty International, <http://www.amnesty.org/ailib/intcam/saudi/>.

75. Yossef Bodansky, "Islamic Anti-Semitism as a Political Instrument," Freeman Center for Strategic Studies, January 1998, <http://www.freeman.org/ m_online/jan98/bodansk.htm>.

76. "Terrorist Financing," report of an independent task force sponsored by the Council on Foreign Relations, October 17, 2002, p. 8, <http://www.cfr.org/ pdf/Terrorist_Financing_TF.pdf>.

77. Michael Isikoff, "9-11 Hijackers: A Saudi Money Trail," *Newsweek*, November 22, 2002, <http://www.msnbc.com/news/838867.asp>.

78. "Saudi Envoy Rejects Terror Allegations," BBC, November 27, 2002, <http://news.bbc.co.uk/2/hi/middle_east/2520005.stm>.

79. Joel Mowbray, "Saudis Behaving Badly," *National Review*, December 20, 2002, <http://www.nationalreview.com/mowbray/mowbray122002.asp>.

80. "Has Someone Been Sitting on the FBI?" *BBC Newsnight*, November 6, 2001, <http://news.bbc.co.uk/1/hi/events/newsnight/1645527.stm>.

81. Jonathan Wells, Jack Meyers and Maggie Mulvihill, "U.S. Ties to Saudi Elite May Be Hurting War on Terrorism," *Boston Herald*, December 10, 2001, <http:// www2.bostonherald.com/news/americas_new_war/saud12102001.htm>.

82. Matthew Levitt, "Combatting Terrorist Financing, Despite the Saudis," Washington Institute for Near East Policy, November 1, 2002, <http://www. washingtoninstitute.org/watch/Policywatch/policywatch2002/673.htm>.

83. "Criminal Intelligence Program: Link Between Al Qaeda and the Diamond Industry," Royal Canadian Mounted Police, July 25, 2002 (updated January 16, 2003), <http://www.rcmp-grc.gc.ca/crim_int/diamond_e.htm>.

84. "9/11 Families Take Groundbreaking Action to Expose Terrorist Financing Schemes, Cut Off Money Pipeline" (news release), August 15, 2002, <http://www.nmlrp.com/practiceareas/911_victims/911action-release_final_8-15-02.pdf>.

85. Ann McFeatters, "Lawsuit Seeks to Cripple Terrorists' Means to Strike," *Pittsburgh Post-Gazette*, August 16, 2002, <http://www.post-gazette.com/nation/20020816suit0816p3.asp>.

86. Wells, Meyers and Mulvihill, op. cit.

87. Maggie Mulvihill, Jack Meyers and Jonathan Wells, "Bush Advisers Cashed in on Saudi Gravy Train," *Boston Herald*, December 11, 2001, <http://www2.bostonherald.com/news/americas_new_war/saud12112001.htm>.

88. Ibid.

89. Melanie Warner, "The Big Guys Work for the Carlyle Group," *Fortune*, March 18, 2002, <http://www.globalresearch.ca/articles/WAR203A.html>.

90. Leslie Wayne, "Elder Bush in Big GOP Cast Toiling for Top Equity Firm," *New York Times*, <http://www.nytimes.com/2001/03/05/politics/05CARL.html>.

91. Warner, op. cit.

92. "Carlyle Group Names First Communications VP," *Holmes Report*, November 19, 2001, <http://www.holmesreport.com/holmestemp/story.cfm?edit_id=1545&typeid=1>.

93. Jim Geraghty, "PR Consultant Claims Bin Laden's Family Contemplating Campaign," States News Service, September 26, 2001.

94. "Hullin Metz Works for Bin Ladens," *O'Dwyer's PR Daily*, November 9, 2001, <http://www.odwyerpr.com/members/archived_stories_2001/november/1109metz.htm>.

95. "Binladen Group May Turn to UK Consultancy," *Holmes Report*, November 26, 2001, <http://www.holmesreport.com/holmestemp/story.cfm?edit_id=1567&typeid=1>.

96. "Saudi Arabia Hires B-M," *O'Dwyer's PR Daily*, October 5, 2001, <http://www.odwyerpr.com/members/archived_stories_2001/october/1005saudi.htm>.

97. "Saudi Arabia Adds to Lobbying Firepower," *O'Dwyer's PR Daily*, January 3, 2003, <http://www.odwyerpr.com/members/washington_report/0103saudi_arabia.htm>.

98. Roger Harrison, "Saudi Arabia's PR Challenge," *Arab News*, <http://www.arabnews.com/Article.asp?ID=19693>.

99. "Saudi Aramco Taps H&K," *O'Dwyer's PR Daily*, January 13, 2003, <http://www.odwyerpr.com/members/washington_report/0113saudi_aramco.htm>.

100. "Gallagher Group Gets Raise from Qorvis," *O'Dwyer's PR Daily*, February 18, 2003, <http://www.odwyerpr.com/members/archived_stories_2003/february/0218gallagher_qorvis.htm> (April 15, 2003).

101. "Initiatives and Actions Taken by the Kingdom of Saudi Arabia to Combat Terrorism," A Report by the Royal Embassy of Saudi Arabia, December 2002, <http://www.opinionjournal.com/soapbox/war_on_terrorism.doc>.

102. "Osama Bin Laden Was Bad Apple, Just Like Jim Jones," *O'Dwyer's PR Daily*, September 10, 2002," <http://www.odwyerpr.com/members/archived_stories_2002/september/0905osama.htm>.

103. "Saudi Embassy Defends Its Stance on Terrorism," *San Antonio Lightning*, July 2002, <http://www.sanantoniolightning.com/stewartjuly.html>.

104. "Defensive Saudis Lash Out at 'Zionist' and U.S. Critics," *Forward*, December 28, 2001, <http://www.forward.com/issues/2001/01.12.28/news6.html>.

105. "Saudis Pay Qorvis $200K a Month," *O'Dwyer's PR Daily*, March 21, 2002, <http://www.odwyerpr.com/members/archived_stories_2002/march/0321qorvis.htm>; "Saudi Arabia Spends $3.8M at Qorvis," *O'Dwyer's PR Daily*, May 16, 2002, <http://www.odwyerpr.com/members/archived_stories_2002/may/0516qorvis.htm>.

106. Bob Garfield, "Zero Stars for Saudi Arabia," *Advertising Age*, May 20, 2002, <http://www.adage.com/news.cms?newsId=35925>.

107. "Qorvis Helps Out on Saudi 'Kidnapping' Controversy," *O'Dwyer's PR Daily*, October 4, 2003, <http://www.odwyerpr.com/members/archived_stories_2003/october/1004qorvis.htm>.

108. Dan Burton, letter to His Royal Highness Prince Bandar bin Sultan bin Abdulaziz, November 21, 2002, <http://www.house.gov/reform/pdf/bandar.02.11.21.pdf>.

109. Philip Shenon, "3 Partners Quit Firm Handling Saudis' PR," *New York Times*, December 6, 2002, <http://www.nytimes.com/2002/12/06/international/middleeast/06SAUD.html>.

4: Doublespeak

1. George Orwell, *A Collection of Essays* (Orlando: Harvest Books, 1970). See also "Politics and the English Language," <http://www.ourcivilisation.com/decline/orwell1.htm>.

2. George Orwell, *1984* (New York: Signet Classic, 1990). See also <http://www.eng.buffalo.edu/~smf7/175/chapp.html>.

3. George W. Bush, State of the Union Address, January 29, 2002, <http://www.whitehouse.gov/news/releases/2002/01/20020129-11.html>.

4. Andrew Marlatt, "Angered by Snubbing, Libya, China, Syria Form Axis of Just As Evil," SatireWire.com, February 1, 2002, <http://www.satirewire.com/news/jan02/axis.shtml>.

5. Department of Defense news briefing (transcript), March 20, 2002, <http://www.defenselink.mil/news/Mar2003/t03202003_t0320sd.html>.

6. Glenn Kessler, "United States Puts a Spin on Coalition Numbers," *Washington Post*, March 21, 2003, p. A29, <http://www.washingtonpost.com/ac2/wp-dyn/A1325-2003Mar20>.

7. "Polls Show European Public Opposed to Iraq War," Reuters, January 30, 2003.

8. William Lutz, *Doublespeak* (New York: HarperPerennial, 1990), pp. 7, 175.

9. "Infinite Justice, Out—Enduring Freedom, In," BBC, September 25, 2001, <http://news.bbc.co.uk/1/hi/world/americas/1563722.stm>.

10. Paul Holmes, "Terminology of War Is Throwing Up a Smokescreen," *PR Week*, April 4, 2003, <http://www.prweek.com/news/news_story.cfm?ID=176363&site=3>.

11. "Rebuilding America's Defenses: Strategy, Forces and Resources for a New American Century," Project for the New American Century, September 2000, pp. iv, v, 2, 4, 7, 14–16, 55, <http://newamericancentury.org/RebuildingAmericasDefenses.pdf>.

12. Ibid.

13. Harlan K. Ullman and James P. Wade, *Shock and Awe: Achieving Rapid Dominance* (NDU Press, October 1996), <http://www.dodccrp.org/shockIndex.html>.

14. Mark J. Conversino, "Shock and Awe: Achieving Rapid Dominance" (book review), *Navy War College Review*, Summer 1998, <http://www.nwc.navy.mil/press/Review/1998/summer/bkr2su98.htm>.

15. Orwell, "Politics and the English Language."

16. Conversino, op. cit.

17. "Iraq Faces Massive U.S. Missile Barrage," CBS News, January 24, 2003, <http://www.cbsnews.com/stories/2003/01/24/eveningnews/main537928.shtml>.

18. Holmes, op. cit.

19. "Language of War" (radio show transcript), America's Defense Monitor, Center for Defense Information, July 29, 1990, <http://www.cdi.org/adm/345/transcript.html>.

20. Bob Kemper, "Agency Wages Media Battle," *Chicago Tribune*, April 7, 2003.

21. "Rumsfeld Warns of 'Marathon' Fight Against Terrorism," U.S. Department of State, September 20, 2001, <http://usinfo.state.gov/topical/pol/terror/01092016.htm>.

22. George W. Bush, remarks following visit to wounded troops at Walter Reed Army Medical Center, Washington, D.C., and National Naval Medical Center, Bethesda, Maryland (transcript), April 11, 2003, <http://www.usembassy.ro/WF/500/eur502.htm>.

5: The Uses of Fear

1. "Terrorism" (encyclopedia entry), Wikipedia.org, <http://www.wikipedia.org/wiki/Terrorism>.

2. "Terror Groups, Governments Use 24/7 News Cycle," *O'Dwyer's PR Daily*, February 12, 2003, <http://www.odwyerpr.com/members/archived_stories_2003/february/0213terrorism_media.htm>.

3. James E. Lukaszewski, "The Media and the Terrorist: A Dance of Death," *Executive Speeches*, June 1987 (Revised 1998), <http://www.e911.com/speeches/mediaandterrorists.html>.

4. Garth S. Jowett and Victoria O'Donnell, *Propaganda and Persuasion* (Thousand Oaks, Calif.: Sage Publications, 1999), p. 42.

5. Ibid., p. 164.

6. Gustave Gilbert, *Nuremberg Diary* (New York: Farrar, Straus and Co., 1947), pp. 278–79.

7. Lary Coppola, "Hummer—the Ultimate 4-wheeler," *Kitsap Business Journal*, May 3, 2003, <http://www.wetapple.com/behindthewheel/articles/2002-05-03-BTW-03.html>.

8. Eric Margolis, "High Oil Prices: The Curse of Saddam," *Toronto Sun*, September 24, 2000, <http://www.twf.org/News/Y2000/0925-OilPrice.html>.

9. Keith Bradsher, "Was Freud a Minivan or SUV Kind of Guy?" *New York Times*, July 17, 2000.

10. Jay Rosen, "When Is a Car a Truck? If Uncle Sam Says So," *New York Times*, November 26, 2002.

11. Gregg Easterbrook, "Axle of Evil" (book review of *High and Mighty*), *New Republic*, January 16, 2003, <http://www.powells.com/review/2003_01_16.html>.

12. Tony Karon, "You Are What You Drive," *Time*, July 17, 2000, <http://www.time.com/time/search/article/0,8599,50060,00.html>.

13. Stephanie Mencimer, "Bumper Mentality," *Washington Monthly*, December 2002, <http://www.washingtonmonthly.com/features/2001/0212.mencimer.html>. See also Myron Levin, "Study Questions Safety of SUVs," *Los Angeles Times*, February 18, 2003, <http://www.latimes.com/business/la-fi-safety18feb18001440,1,2402829.story>; Ricardo Alonso-Zaldivar, "Automaker Data Say SUVs Are Riskier," *Los Angeles Times*, February 26, 2003, <http://www.latimes.com/la-fi-suv26feb26001431.story>.

14. Easterbrook, op. cit.

15. Paul Wilborn, "Hummer Sales Plow Over Criticism of Gas Mileage, View-Blocking Bulk," Associated Press/*Naples Daily News*, February 4, 2003, <http://www.naplesnews.com/03/02/business/d890397a.htm>.

16. Phil Patton, "Here Come the Car Shrinks," *Fortune*, March 5, 2002, <http://www.fortune.com/fortune/personalfortune/articles/0,15114,373444,00.html>.

17. Danny Hakim, "In Their Hummers, Right Beside Uncle Sam," *New York Times*, April 4, 2003, <http://www.nytimes.com/2003/04/05/business/05AUTO.html>.

18. Ibid.

19. Douglas Quenqua, "Guns or Butter?" *PR Week*, March 11, 2002, <http://www.prweek.com/news/news_story.cfm?ID=139666&site=3>.

20. "Senators to Push for Alaska Oil Drilling This Week," Reuters, April 11, 2002, <http://www.planetark.org/dailynewsstory.cfm/newsid/15418/newsDate/11-Apr-2002/story.htm>.

21. Donald F. Kettl, "'West Wing' Fallout," *Governing Magazine*, June 2002, p. 12.

22. William J. Kole, "Terrorism Haunts Nuke Delegates," Associated Press, September 17, 2001.

23. "More Than Strong Fences" (advertisement), reproduced in *O'Dwyer's PR Daily*, January 30, 2002, <http://www.odwyerpr.com/members/archived_stories_2002/january/0130nei.htm>.

24. Julie Hinds, "TV Spots Heating Up SUV Fight," Auto.com, January 9, 2003, <http://www.auto.com/industry/nusuv9_20030109.htm>. See also <http://www.detroitproject.com>.

25. "PR Needed to Keep Consumers Spending," *Jack O'Dwyer's Newsletter*, vol. 34, no. 38, September 26, 2001, p. 7.

26. Chuck Kelly, "Spiritual Patriotism," *Star Tribune* (Minneapolis/St. Paul), November 18, 2001.

27. President Bush: Job Ratings, *Newsweek* poll conducted by Princeton Survey Research Associates, summarized on PollingReport.com, <http://www.pollingreport.com/BushJob.htm>.

28. Ibid.

29. Ron Faucheaux, "Ups, Downs of Presidential Popularity," *Campaigns & Elections*, February 1, 2002, <http://www.campaignline.com/commentary/index.cfm?id=70>.

30. Ibid.

31. Angie Cannon, "Taking Liberties," *U.S. News & World Report*, May 12, 2003, <http://www.usnews.com/usnews/issue/030512/misc/12moussaoui.htm>.

32. Deputy Secretary of Defense Paul Wolfowitz, interview with Thabet El-Bardicy, Middle East Broadcasting Center, December 6, 2001, <http://www.defenselink.mil/news/Dec2001/t12102001_t1206mbc.html>.

33. "'Islam is Peace' Says President," remarks at Islamic Center of Washington, D.C., September 17, 2001, <http://www.whitehouse.gov/news/releases/2001/09/20010917-11.html>.

34. Ann Coulter, "This Is War," *National Review*, September 13, 2001, <http://www.nationalreview.com/coulter/coulter091301.shtml>.

35. Jonah Goldberg, "L'Affaire Coulter," *National Review*, October 3, 2001, <http://www.nationalreview.com/nr_comment/nr_comment100301.shtml>.

36. "U.S. Attack News," Markazdawa.org (website), <http://www.markazdawa.org/English/EVENTS/US/index.html> (October 7, 2001).

37. "President Distances Himself From Comments About Islam," *Christian Times*, January 3, 2003, <http://www.christiantimes.com/Articles/Articles%

20Jan03/Art_Jan03_12.html>; "Nov. 11 Statement by Pat Robertson on *The 700 Club*" (news release), PatRobertson.com, November 14, 2003, <http://www.patrobertson.com/PressReleases/bushresponse2.asp>.

38. *Religion and Ethics Newsweekly*, show #509 (transcript), PBS, November 2, 2001, <http://www.pbs.org/wnet/religionandethics/transcripts/509.html>.

39. Don Feder, "Why We Keep Getting Islam Wrong," speech to the Christian Coalition Symposium on Islam, February 15, 2003, <http://www.donfeder.com/filecabinet//02152003.txt>.

40. Al Kamen, "Sticker Shock," *Washington Post*, January 31, 2003, p. A25, <http://www.washingtonpost.com/ac2/wp-dyn/A3956-2003Jan30>.

41. Jay Bookman, "Liberals, Report to Re-education," *Atlanta Journal-Constitution*, February 14, 2002, <http://www.accessatlanta.com/ajc/opinion/bookman/2002/021402.html>.

42. "McInnis Presses Forward With 'ELF' Subpoena" (news release), October 2, 2001, <http://www.house.gov/mcinnis/pr011002.htm>.

43. Ben White, "Will the Environment Become a Casualty of the Terrorist Attacks?" *Grist*, September 15, 2001, <http://www.gristmagazine.com/grist/muck/muck091501.asp?source=daily>.

44. Mary Mostert, "Was It Osama Bin Laden or Is He Just a Minor Player?" Reagan Information Interchange, September 13, 2001, <http://www.reagan.com/HotTopics.main/document-9.13.2001.8.html> (September 21, 2001).

45. "War Against Eco-terrorists," *Washington Times*, October 7, 2001, <http://www.washtimes.com/op-ed/20011007-55556656.htm>.

46. Tom Curry, "Saddam, Bin Laden Become Political Props," MSNBC, November 7, 2001, <http://www.msnbc.com/news/654184.asp>.

47. Dana Milbank, "A Double-Barrelled Attack on Daschle," *Washington Post*, November 9, 2001, p. A6, <http://www.washingtonpost.com/ac2/wp-dyn/A64965-2001Nov8>.

48. William Bennett, open letter, "Week in Review" section, *New York Times*, March 10, 2002.

49. Dan Eggen and Dana Priest, "Bush Aides Seek to Contain Furor," *Washington Post*, May 17, 2002, p. A1, <http://www.washingtonpost.com/ac2/wp-dyn/A30219-2002May16>. See also Philip Shenon, "FBI Knew for Years About Terror Pilot Training," *New York Times*, May 18, 2002, <http://www.nytimes.com/2002/05/18/politics/18FLIG.html>.

Notes

50. "Background: Hijack Warnings," *NewsHour*, PBS, May 17, 2002, <http://www.pbs.org/newshour/bb/terrorism/jan-june02/bkgddots_5-17.html>.

51. *The Beltway Boys*, Fox News (transcript #051801cb.257), May 19, 2002.

52. Dan Balz, "Bush and GOP Defend White House Response," *Washington Post*, May 18, 2002, p. A1, <http://www.washingtonpost.com/ac2/wp-dyn/A35718-2002May17>. See also Brendan Nyhan, "Axing the Tough Questions," Salon.com, May 21, 2002, <http://www.spinsanity.org/columns/20020521.html>.

53. Ellen Sorokin, "NEA Delivers History Lesson," *Washington Times*, August 19, 2002, <http://www.washtimes.com/national/20020819-34549100.htm>.

54. Oliver North, "Terrorism in the Classroom," *Washington Times*, August 25, 2002, <http://www.washtimes.com/commentary/20020825-9252640.htm>.

55. Lisa De Pasquale, "'Blame America First' Teaches Youth to Embrace Islam," *Washington Times*, September 8, 2002, <http://www.cblpolicyinstitute.org/sept11ann.htm>.

56. George F. Will, "The Feel-Good Approach to Sept. 11," *Washington Post*, August 25, 2002, p. B7, <http://www.washingtonpost.com/ac2/wp-dyn/A55511-2002Aug23>. See also Brendan Nyhan, "The Big NEA–Sept. 11 Lie," Salon.com, September 5, 2002, <http://www.spinsanity.org/columns/20020905.html>; Bob Somerby, "Slime the Teachers Well!" *Daily Howler*, August 28, 2002, <http://www.dailyhowler.com/dh082802.shtml>.

57. "Surveillance Under the 'USA/Patriot' Act," American Civil Liberties Union, <http://archive.aclu.org/issues/privacy/USAPA_surveillance.html>.

58. "President Issues Military Order," Office of the Press Secretary, U.S. White House, November 13, 2001, <http://www.whitehouse.gov/news/releases/2001/11/20011113-27.html>.

59. "End-Running the Bill of Rights," *Washington Post*, November 16, 2001, p. A46.

60. "The Contras, Cocaine, and Covert Operations," National Security Archive Electronic Briefing Book No. 2, <http://www.gwu.edu/~nsarchiv/NSAEBB/NSAEBB2/nsaebb2.htm#3>. See also Arthur L. Liman, "Hostile Witness," *Washington Post Magazine*, August 16, 1998, <http://www.washingtonpost.com/wp-srv/national/longterm/irancontra/contra1.htm>.

61. Cynthia L. Webb, "The Pentagon's PR Play," *Washington Post*, May 21, 2003, <http://www.washingtonpost.com/wp-dyn/articles/A19272-2003May21.html>.

62. "Freedom in 30 Seconds" (transcript), *On the Media*, July 5, 2002, <http://www.wnyc.org/onthemedia/transcripts_070502_freedom.html>.

63. "Attorney General Reno's FOIA Memorandum," U.S. Department of Justice, October 4, 1993, <http://www.usdoj.gov/oip/foia_updates/Vol_XIV_3/page3.htm>.

64. "New Attorney General FOIA Memorandum Issued," U.S. Department of Justice, October 12, 2001, <http://www.usdoj.gov/oip/foiapost/2001foiapost19.htm>.

65. "Ashcroft Tells Agencies to Resist FOIA Releases," *Secrecy News*, Federation of American Scientists, October 17, 2001, <http://www.fas.org/sgp/news/secrecy/2001/10/101701.html>.

66. Jonathan H. Adler, "How the EPA Helps Terrorists," *National Review Online*, September 27, 2001, <http://www.nationalreview.com/comment/comment-adlerprint092701.html>.

67. "Would You Want Detailed Information About Chemical Plants in Your Hometown Publicized?" Competitive Enterprise Institute, January 10, 2002, <http://www.cei.org/gencon/003,02283.cfm>.

68. Letter to Hon. Janet Reno, Working Group on Community Right-to-Know, August 14, 2000, <http://www.ehw.org/Chemical_Accidents/CHEM_Reno Ltr.htm>.

69. "Access to Government Information Post September 11th," OMB Watch, February 1, 2002, <http://www.ombwatch.org/article/articleview/213/1/1/>.

70. "Responding to Chemical Attacks," from *Terrorism: Questions and Answers*, <http://www.terrorismanswers.com/security/chemical.html>.

71. "Seven Good Reasons to Stand Up for Information Freedom on Bioweapons Research," Sunshine Project USA, October 30, 2001, <http://www.sunshine-project.org/publications/pr301001.html> (June 5, 2002).

72. "Critique of the Codeword Compartment in the CIA" (intelligence monograph), Center for the Study of Intelligence, Central Intelligence Agency, March 1977, <http://www.fas.org/sgp/othergov/codeword.html>.

73. Eleanor Hill, Joint Inquiry Staff Statement, U.S. House and Senate Intelligence Committee joint hearing, October 17, 2002, <http://www.fas.org/irp/congress/2002_hr/101702hill.html>.

6: The Air War

1. The Jeremy Glick who appeared on *The O'Reilly Factor* is the son of Barry Glick, a 51-year-old worker at Port Authority. He is not related to Jeremy Glick, the 31-year-old passenger of Flight 93 who is believed to have fought the hijackers and prevented them from crashing the plane into its intended target.

2. *The O'Reilly Factor*, February 4, 2003 (transcript #020404cb.256, available on the LexisNexis news database). See also <http://www.thismodernworld.com/weblog/mtarchives/week_2003_02_02.html>.

3. "Did Anyone Just See O'Reilly Tear Into Jeremy Glick?" Free Republic.com, <http://www.freerepublic.com/focus/news/836052/posts>.

4. Bill O'Reilly, "Using Quasi-Prostitutes to Sell Sneakers," Fox News, February 25, 2003, <http://www.foxnews.com/story/0,2933,79542,00.html>.

5. Media Research Center, IRS Form 990, 2001, <http://documents.guidestar.org/2001/541/429/2001-541429009-1-9.pdf>; Fairness and Accuracy in Reporting, IRS Form 990 for fiscal year ending June 30, 2002, <http://documents.guidestar.org/2002/133/392/2002-133392362-1-9.pdf>.

6. Jim Rutenberg and Bill Carter, "Network Coverage a Target of Fire from Conservatives," *New York Times*, November 7, 2001, <http://www.nytimes.com/2001/11/07/politics/07MEDI.html>.

7. Press briefing by Ari Fleischer (transcript), White House Office of the Press Secretary, September 26, 2001, <http://www.whitehouse.gov/news/releases/2001/09/20010926-5.html>.

8. Testimony of Attorney General John Ashcroft, Senate Committee on the Judiciary, December 6, 2001, <http://www.justice.gov/ag/speeches/2001/1206transcriptsenatejudiciarycommittee.htm>.

9. Dennis Pluchinsky, "They Heard It All Here, and That's the Trouble," *Washington Post*, June 16, 2002, p. B3, <http://www.washingtonpost.com/ac2/wp-dyn/A54650-2002Jun14>.

10. Roy Greenlade, "Their Master's Voice," *Guardian* (UK), February 17, 2003, <http://media.guardian.co.uk/iraqandthemedia/story/0,12823,897313,00.html>.

11. "The New York Post Captures the Mood of the Extreme Right," *Global Beat*, Center for War, Peace and the News Media, New York University, February 17–24, 2003, <http://www.nyu.edu/globalbeat/index021703.html>.

12. Ciar Byrne, "Sun's French Stunt Called 'Disgusting,'" *Guardian* (UK), February 21, 2003, <http://media.guardian.co.uk/iraqandthemedia/story/0,12823,900179,00.html>.

13. Sam Keen, "To Create an Enemy" (poem), cited in "Healing the Enemy 2001" (sermon), preached at Grace North Church, Berkeley, Calif., January 21, 2001, <http://www.apocryphile.net/homily/sermons/enemy01.html>.

14. Bill Carter, "MSNBC Cancels Donahue," February 25, 2003, <http://www.nytimes.com/2003/02/25/business/media/25CND-PHIL.html>.

15. Rick Ellis, "Commentary: The Surrender of MSNBC," AllYourTV.com, February 25, 2003, <http://www.allyourtv.com/0203season/news/02252003donahue.html>.

16. "GE, Microsoft Bring Bigotry to Life," FAIR Action Alert, February 12, 2003, <http://www.fair.org/activism/msnbc-savage.html>.

17. John Schwartz and Geraldine Fabrikant, "War Puts Radio Giant on the Defensive," *New York Times*, March 31, 2003, <http://www.nytimes.com/2003/03/31/business/media/31RADI.html>.

18. "Dixie Chicks' 'Top of the World Tour' a Great Success" (news release), Clear Channel Entertainment, Inc., March 7, 2003, <http://biz.yahoo.com/bw/030307/75279_1.html>.

19. "DJs Suspended for Playing Dixie Chicks," *Washington Post*, May 6, 2003, <http://www.washingtonpost.com/wp-dyn/articles/A19571-2003May6.html>.

20. "Treatment of Dixie Chicks by Some Radio Stations Raises Troubling Issues," *Citizen Times* (Asheville, N.C.), May 2, 2003, <http://cgi.citizen-times.com/cgi-bin/story/editorial/34115>.

21. John Mainelli, "Tough Talkers," *New York Post*, March 21, 2003, <http://www.nypost.com/entertainment/71400.htm>.

22. Todd Gitlin, "The Pro-War Post," *American Prospect*, April 2003, p. 43.

23. Michael Getler, "Worth More Than a One-liner," *Washington Post*, October 6, 2002, p. B6, <http://www.washingtonpost.com/ac2/wp-dyn/A45771-2002Oct4>.

24. Ira Teinowitz, "Battle Rages Over Anti-war TV Commercials," *Advertising Age*, February 24, 2003, <http://www.adage.com/news.cms?newsId=37202>.

25. Nat Ives, "MTV Refuses Antiwar Commercial," *New York Times*, March 13, 2003, <http://www.nytimes.com/2003/03/13/business/media/13ADCO.html>.

26. Claude Moisy, "The Foreign News Flow in the Information Age," Discussion Paper D-23, Joan Shorenstein Center on the Press, Politics and Public Policy, Harvard University, November 1996, p. 4, <http://www.ksg.harvard.edu/presspol/publications/pdfs/62062_D-23.pdf>.

27. Mark Fitzgerald, "TV Trounced Newspapers During Iraq War," *Editor & Publisher*, April 30, 2003, <http://www.editorandpublisher.com/editorandpublisher/headlines/article_display.jsp?vnu_content_id=1876975>.

28. Ibid.

29. Josh Getlin, "All-News Channels Find Big Audience," *Los Angeles Times*, April 5, 2003, <http://www.latimes.com/news/custom/timespoll/la-war-media5apr05,1,6903445.story?coll=la%2Dnews%2Dtimes%5Fpoll>.

30. Eric Deggans, "Pride and Prejudice," *St. Petersburg Times*, April 25, 2003, <http://www.sptimes.com/2003/04/25/Floridian/Pride_and_prejudice.shtml>.

31. Allison Romano, "CNN Out-Foxed in War Coverage," *Broadcasting & Cable*, March 20, 2003, <http://www.broadcastingcable.com/index.asp?layout=story_stocks&articleId=CA286394>.

32. Jim Rutenberg, "Cable's War Coverage Suggests a New 'Fox Effect' on Television," *New York Times*, April 16, 2003, <http://www.nytimes.com/2003/04/16/international/worldspecial/16FOX.html>.

33. Moisy, op. cit.

34. Ibid.

35. Justin Lewis, Sut Jhally and Michael Morgan, "The Gulf War: A Study of the Media, Public Opinion and Public Knowledge," Centre for the Study of Communication, University of Massachusetts/Amherst, February 1991, <http://www-unix.oit.umass.edu/~commdept/resources/gulfwar.html>.

36. Neil Cavuto, "American First, Journalist Second," *Fox News*, March 28, 2003, <http://www.foxnews.com/story/0,2933,82504,00.html>.

37. Chuck Barney, "Fox Offering More News Talk Than News," *Contra Costa Times*, April 10, 2003, <http://www.bayarea.com/mld/cctimes/entertainment/columnists/chuck_barney/5601320.htm>.

38. *Hardball with Chris Matthews*, MSNBC, April 2, 2003 (transcript #040201cb.461).

39. Peter Johnson, "Media's War Footing Looks Solid," *USA Today*, February 17, 2003, p. 1D.

40. "Operation Iraqi Freedom" (transcript #032606cb.455), MSNBC, March 26, 2003.

41. "Press, freedom of the," *The Columbia Encyclopedia*, 6th ed. (New York: Columbia University Press, 2003), <http://www.bartleby.com/65/pr/press-fr.html>.

42. "How the War Changed the Way Military Conflicts Are Reported," *University Times* (University of Pittsburgh), vol. 32, no. 21, June 22, 2000, <http://www.pitt.edu/utimes/issues/32/000622/15.html>.

43. Daniel Hallin, "Vietnam on Television," *The Encyclopedia of Television*, Museum of Broadcast Communications, <http://www.museum.tv/archives/etv/V/htmlV/vietnamonte/vietnamonte.htm>.

44. Namrata Savoor, "Persian Gulf War Press Pool Worked Well in Some Ways," Newseum.org, July 16, 2001, <http://www.newseum.org/warstories/exhibitinfo/newsstory.asp?DocumentID=14402>.

45. Peter Turnley, "The Unseen Gulf War," World Association for Christian Communication, <http://www.wacc.org.uk/publications/action/250/unseen_war.html>.

46. Peter Johnson, "Who Won, and Who Lost, in the Media Battle," *USA Today*, April 13, 2003, <http://www.usatoday.com/life/world/iraq/2003-04-13-media-mix_x.htm>.

47. Robert Jensen, "The Military's Media," *Progressive*, May 20, 2003, <http://www.progressive.org/may03/jen0503.html>.

48. Douglas Quenqua, "Pentagon PA Staff Helping Out Embedded Reporters," *PR Week*, March 31, 2003, <http://www.prweek.com/news/news_story.cfm?ID=175623&site=3>.

49. Douglas Holt, "Media Face Difficult Call on Reporters in War Zone," *Chicago Tribune*, March 12, 2003.

50. "NBC, ABC Pull Reporters from Baghdad After Comments Indicating War," Associated Press, March 17, 2003, <http://www.bayarea.com/mld/mercurynews/entertainment/television/5414596.htm>. See also Jim Rutenberg, "US News Organizations Tell Employees to Leave Baghdad," *New York Times*, March 19, 2003, <http://www.nytimes.com/2003/03/19/national/19MEDI.html>.

51. Allesandra Stanley, "After a Lengthy Buildup, an Anticlimactic Strike," *New York Times*, March 20, 2003, <http://www.nytimes.com/2003/03/20/international/worldspecial/20WATC.html>.

52. Jane Perlez with Jim Rutenberg, "U.S. Courts Network It Once Described as 'All Osama,'" *New York Times*, March 20, 2003, <http://www.nytimes.com/2003/03/20/international/worldspecial/20JAZE.html>.

53. Jensen, op. cit.

54. Ibid.

55. Howard Kurtz, "For Media After Iraq, a Case of Shell Shock," *Washington Post*, April 28, 2003, p. A1.

56. David Folkenflik, "Fox News Defends Its 'Patriotic' Coverage," *Baltimore Sun*, April 2, 2003, <http://www.baltimoresun.com/entertainment/tv/bal-to.tvradio02apr02,0,6090522.column?coll=bal%2Dtv%2Dutility>.

57. Katie Delahaye Paine, "Army Intelligence," *Measurement Standard*, March 28, 2003, <http://www.themeasurementstandard.com/issues/303/eng/painemilitary303.asp>.

58. Ariel Sabar, "Military Crews Capture Images from Front Line," *Baltimore Sun*, April 18, 2003, <http://www.sunspot.net/news/local/annearundel/bal-ar.camera18apr18,0,164731.story?coll=bal-local-arundel>.

59. Ibid.

7: As Others See Us

1. "President Bush Announces Combat Operations in Iraq Have Ended," White House Office of the Press Secretary, May 1, 2003, <http://www.whitehouse.gov/news/releases/2003/05/iraq/20030501-15.html>. See also Maura Reynolds and Anna R. Gorham, "After the War," *Los Angeles Times*, May 2, 2003.

2. William Douglas, "Bush's 'Great Image,'" *Newsday*, May 2, 2003, p. A6.

3. Ken Fireman, "Dems: Landing Cost $1M," *Newsday*, May 8, 2003, p. A43.

4. Julie Mason, "Critics Cry, Comics Scoff at Bush's Carrier Rally," *Houston Chronicle*, May 8, 2003, p. A3.

5. Mike Allen, "Ship Carrying Bush Delayed Return," *Washington Post*, May 8, 2003, p. A29.

6. Scott Lindlaw, "Accommodating TV-friendly Presidential Visit Caused a Few Changes in Navy Carrier's Routine," Associated Press, May 2, 2003.

7. Douglas, op. cit.

8. Ibid.

9. Tom Shales, "Aboard the Lincoln, A White House Spectacular," *Washington Post*, May 2, 2003, p. C1, <http://www.washingtonpost.com/wp-dyn/articles/A3823-2003May2.html>.

10. "President Bush Announces Combat Operations in Iraq Have Ended," op. cit.

11. Eric Boehlert, "Sanitized for Our Protection," Salon.com, April 11, 2003, <http://www.salon.com/news/feature/2003/04/11/images/print.html>.

12. Lisa Marshall, "Boulder Man Operated on Recently Rescued POW in Germany," *Daily Camera* (Boulder, Colo.), April 5, 2003, <http://www.dailycamera.com/bdc/county_news/article/0,1713,BDC_2423_1866804,00.html>.

13. Paul Holmes, "The Way the US is Viewing This War Will Have a Lasting Impact on How the World Views the US," *PR Week*, April 7, 2003.

14. "Cluster Bombs Are Indiscriminate and Morally Indefensible," letter by international relief agencies, *Independent* (UK), April 7, 2003.

15. Ibid.

16. Lindsey Hilsum, "Chaos and Denial in Baghdad," *Christian Science Monitor*, April 7, 2003, p. 1.

17. Anthony DePalma, "A Nation At War," *New York Times*, April 8, 2003, p. B1.

18. "US Military Sees No Indication Cluster Munitions Used in Hilla," Agence France Presse, April 2, 2003.

19. Ibid.

20. "Iraq: Civilians Under Fire," Amnesty International, March 8, 2003, <http://web.amnesty.org/pages/irq-engmde140712003>.

21. "Numbers and Estimates from Iraq War," Associated Press, April 4, 2003.

22. Benny Evangelista, "Kevlar Saving Lives, Minimizing Wounds in Iraq," *San Francisco Chronicle*, April 7, 2003, p. E1.

23. Don Wycliff, "No Hiding the Deadly Face of War," *Chicago Tribune*, May 1, 2003, p. 23.

24. Greg Miller, "Head of Joint Chiefs Defends Use of Cluster Bombs in Iraq," *Los Angeles Times*, April 26, 2003, p. 8.

25. Michael Weisskopf, "Civilian Deaths: the Bombs That Keep on Killing," *Time*, May 3, 2003, <http://www.time.com/time/magazine/article/0,9171,1101030512-449440,00.html>.

Notes

26. Miller, op. cit.
27. John Otis, "Arab Media Accused of War Bias," *Houston Chronicle,* April 5, 2003, p. A25.
28. Reed Hunt, "Television War vs. Television Peace," *Broadcasting & Cable,* April 14, 2003, <http://www.broadcastingcable.com/index.asp?layout=story_stocks&articleId=CA291889>.
29. Rami Khouri, "Not a Pretty Picture," Alternet.org, March 31, 2003, <http://www.alternet.org/story.html?StoryID=15509>.
30. "Al-Jazeera Tops Net Search Requests," Associated Press, April 1, 2003, <http://www.msnbc.com/news/894112.asp>.
31. Byron Acohido, "Hack Attack on Al-Jazeera Raises Questions," *USA Today,* March 30, 2003, <http://www.usatoday.com/tech/world/iraq/2003-03-30-iraq-web_x.htm>.
32. Robert Fisk, "Raw, Painful, Devastating War," *Seattle Post-Intelligencer,* March 28, 2003, <http://seattlepi.nwsource.com/opinion/114604_fisk28.shtml>.
33. David Pallister, "Mystery Sheikh Fuels Saudi Jitters," *Guardian* (UK), December 15, 2001, <http://www.guardian.co.uk/afghanistanb/story/0,1284,619191,00.html>.
34. Moulay Hicham El Alaoui, "Prescription for Disaster," *Le Monde,* July 6, 2002.
35. Moulay Hicham El Alaoui, "Politics and Governance in Islam," talk given at Princeton University, September 2002. Full disclosure: Moulay Hicham and Sheldon Rampton were student acquaintances at Princton University, and Rampton encountered the passages cited here while helping to develop the Prince's website (www.moulayhicham.net).
36. "Impressions of Holy War," ABC News, March 31, 2003, <http://abcnews.go.com/sections/world/Primetime/iraq_crusade030331.html>.

Index

Index

Index

Index

Media war, 161–166
    Combat Camera, 187–188
    Gulf War II, 173–181
    overcoming "Vietnam Syndrome,"
        182–187
    patriotism police, 166–173
Meet the Press, 95
Mein Kampf (Hitler), 135
Meyers, Jack, 105
Middle East Watch, 74
Military doublespeak, 118–119
Miller, Greg, 197–198
Miller, Judith, 57
Moisy, Claude, 173
Moran, Paul, 50
Morocco, 30
Motley, Ron, 104
Mowbray, Joel, 103
MSNBC Network, 119, 169–170, 174,
    176–181
Mubarak, Hosni, 204
Mueller, Robert, 93
Mujahedin-e-Khalq (MEK), 100
Mulvihill, Maggie, 104
Murdoch, Rupert, 168–169
Murkowski, Frank, 140–141
Murphy, Kim, 201–202
Muslims, as enemy, 145–148
Myers, Richard B., Gen., 186, 197
Mylroie, Laurie, 57–58

Nagasaki, 123–124
Nathanson, Marc, 13
National Drug Council, 141
National Education Association,
    151–152
National Journal, 141
National Review, 146
National Security Archive (NSA), 15
NATO, 117
Nayirah testimony, 72–75
New Republic, 58
Newsweek, 7, 24, 38
New Yorker, 50–51

New York Observer, 59–60
New York Post, 168
New York Times, 3, 12, 29, 31–32, 37,
    41, 49, 54, 60, 63, 66–67,
    92–93, 107–108, 112, 167, 192,
    195
"Next Chapter" (TV show), 31–32
9/11 Families United to Bankrupt
    Terrorism, 104
Nixon, Richard, 144–145
North, Oliver, 186
North Korea, 89, 114–116
Nuclear Energy Institute, 141
Nuclear Regulatory Commission,
    158–159
Nuremberg Diary (Gilbert),
    136–137

Observer (London), 99
O'Donnell, Victoria, 135
O'Dwyer's PR Daily, 108–109, 133,
    142
Office of Global Communications
    (OGC), 38
Office of Strategic Influence (OSI),
    49, 66–68
Open Dialogue (website), 32–33
Operation Desert Storm, 42–43,
    76–78, 80, 137, 175,
    183–184
Operation Iraqi Freedom, 4, 6, 116
O'Reilly, Bill, 162–166
The O'Reilly Factor, 162–166
Orwell, George, 113–114, 124

Pace, Peter, Gen., 61
Paine, Katie Delahaye, 187
Palast, Greg, 103
Palestinians, 29
Patriotism police, 166–173
"Patterns of Global Terrorism" (U.S.
    State Dept.), 99–103
Pentagon, 5–6, 154, 183
    and Combat Camera, 187–188

Index

About the Authors

Sheldon Rampton and John Stauber both work for the Center for Media & Democracy, a nonprofit organization that Stauber founded in 1993 to monitor and expose deceptive public relations campaigns and other propaganda sponsored by corporations and governments. They write and edit the Center's quarterly publication, *PR Watch*. They have co-authored three previous books: *Toxic Sludge Is Good for You!: Lies, Damn Lies and the Public Relations Industry* (1995); *Mad Cow U.S.A.: Could the Nightmare Happen Here?* (1997); and *Trust Us, We're Experts!: How Industry Manipulates Science and Gambles with Your Future* (2001).

John Stauber is a longtime activist who has worked with public-interest, consumer, family-farm, environmental and community organizations at the local, state and national levels. Before founding the Center, he worked for five years for the Foundation on Economic Trends, a Washington, D.C., nonprofit organization, researching possible health and economic impacts of recombinant bovine growth hormone (rBGH) and organizing concerned citizens and farmers. Born in 1953, he is married and lives in Madison, Wisconsin.

Sheldon Rampton is a graduate of Princeton University and has a diverse background as a newspaper reporter, activist and author. In college, he studied writing under Joyce Carol Oates, E. L. Doctorow and John McPhee. In addition to books authored with John Stauber, he is the co-author (with Liz Chilsen) of the 1998 book *Friends In Deed: the Story of U.S.-Nicaragua Sister Cities*. Prior to joining the Center for Media & Democracy, he worked for the Wisconsin Coordinating Council on Nicaragua (www.wccnica.org) on the NICA Fund, a project that since 1992 has channeled $10 million in loans from U.S. investors to support economic development efforts in low-income Central American communities.

For further information about the authors, including archived copies of *PR Watch*, visit the PR Watch website (www.prwatch.org) or contact:

Center for Media & Democracy
520 University Avenue, Suite 310
Madison, WI 53703
Phone: (608) 260-9713